LIVING TRUSTS
MADE E-Z!

by
Valerie Hope Goldstein

E·Z LEGAL FORMS®

Deerfield Beach, Florida
www.e-zlegal.com

NOTICE:

THIS PRODUCT IS NOT INTENDED TO PROVIDE LEGAL ADVICE. IT CONTAINS GENERAL INFORMATION FOR EDUCATIONAL PURPOSES ONLY. PLEASE CONSULT AN ATTORNEY IN ALL LEGAL MATTERS. THIS PRODUCT WAS NOT PREPARED BY A PERSON LICENSED TO PRACTICE LAW IN THIS STATE.

APR 2 8 2000   3 9082 07612 9041

Living Trusts Made E-Z™
Copyright 1999 E-Z Legal Forms, Inc.
Printed in the United States of America

E·Z LEGAL FORMS®

384 South Military Trail Deerfield Beach, FL 33442
Tel. 954-480-8933 Fax 954-480-8906
http://www.e-zlegal.com/
All rights reserved.
Distributed by E-Z Legal Forms, Inc.

1 2 3 4 5 6 7 8 9 10   CPC   R   10 9 8 7 6 5 4 3 2

This publication is designed to provide accurate and authoritative information in regard to subject matter covered. It is sold with the understanding that neither the publisher nor author is engaged in rendering legal, accounting, or other professional services. If legal advice or other expert assistance is required, the services of a competent professional should be sought. From: *A Declaration of Principles jointly adopted by a Committee of the American Bar Association and a Committee of Publishers.*

Living Trusts Made E-Z™
Written by Valerie Hope Goldstein

Important Notice

Limited warranty and disclaimer

Table of contents

How to use this guide

E-Z Legal's Made E-Z™ Guides can help you achieve an important legal objective conveniently, efficiently and economically. But it is important to properly use this guide if you are to avoid later difficulties.

◆ Carefully read all information, warnings and disclaimers concerning the legal forms in this guide. If after thorough examination you decide that you have circumstances that are not covered by the forms in this guide, or you do not feel confident about preparing your own documents, consult an attorney.

◆ Complete each blank on each legal form. Do not skip over inapplicable blanks or lines intended to be completed. If the blank is inapplicable, mark "N/A" or "None" or use a dash. This shows you have not overlooked the item.

◆ Always use pen or type on legal documents—never use pencil.

◆ Avoid erasures and "cross-outs" on final documents. Use photocopies of each document as worksheets, or as final copies. All documents submitted to the court must be printed on one side only.

◆ Correspondence forms may be reproduced on your own letterhead if you prefer.

◆ Whenever legal documents are to be executed by a partnership or corporation, the signatory should designate his or her title.

◆ It is important to remember that on legal contracts or agreements between parties all terms and conditions must be clearly stated. Provisions may not be enforceable unless in writing. All parties to the agreement should receive a copy.

◆ Instructions contained in this guide are for your benefit and protection, so follow them closely.

◆ You will find a glossary of useful terms at the end of this guide. Refer to this glossary if you encounter unfamiliar terms.

◆ Always keep legal documents in a safe place and in a location known to your spouse, family, personal representative or attorney.

Introduction to Living Trusts Made E-Z™

Don't give the probate court control of your assets! By depending on a will to protect your loved ones, you do just that. A living trust eliminates the costs and delays of probate and ensures that your loved ones receive their inheritance when they need it most and as you planned. A living trust is a simple, inexpensive legal alternative that can eliminate costly estate probate charges and attorneys' fees.

An excellent option for many, the living trust shortens the time it takes to distribute funds to your heirs by months or even years. It makes it difficult to contest or overturn your wishes regarding the disposition of your estate and, the living trust remains completely private, rather than a public document open to inspection. Finally, your living trust may be revoked at any time or amended whenever you change your mind.

Careful planning can help resolve many of the problems associated with a traditional will and after-death settlements. In addition, if you become incapacitated, your successor trustee may handle your financial affairs without having the court appoint a guardian or conservator unfamiliar to you or your family. A living trust may be used alone or in addition to a will.

With direct and clear answers, Living Trust Made E-Z™ walks you through the process of establishing a living trust. Determine if a living trust is right for you and, if so, what type of trust will best protect your assets. This guide contains the forms, definitions, and contacts to help you organize and complete your living trust. Don't hesitate. Explore your options and protect your assets and your loved ones' best interests—we've made it E-Z!

Nine good reasons to have a living trust

1

Chapter 1

Nine good reasons to have a living trust

What you'll find in this chapter:

➡ Advantages of a living trust

➡ About the revocable living trust

➡ How to select your trustee

➡ Trustee responsibilities

➡ Differences between a will and a living trust

Picture this: One day you purchase a giant safe. You put your most valuable belongings in it—cash, real estate, stocks, bonds, mutual funds, airplanes, the works. You give the combination to a trusted friend or family member, who guards the assets inside the safe and lets you use what you want when you want.

E-Z TIP

You don't have to be rich to establish a trust. In fact, you can set up a trust with just one dollar and add your assets to it at a later date. Trusts can help everyone avoid probate, if handled correctly.

Eventually you pass away, leaving your loved ones behind. The person watching the safe unlocks it and, just as you instructed, distributes the assets inside the safe to your family members. There is no waiting, no public record, no estate attorney to bill your family, no taxes to pay, no fighting it out in court. Best of all, no one

---

outside your family can get a peek at your estate by looking at a copy of your will. There is no will.

Sound too good to be true? Not only is the above possible, it's advisable if you have personal assets totalling more than your state probate limit ($30,000 in some states, $60,000 in others). And it can all be accomplished by setting up a revocable living trust.

What is a living trust?

A living trust is a legal agreement in which a person owning property, the *grantor,* hands over legal title to his or her property to a second person, the *trustee,* who manages it while the grantor is alive. As grantor, you do not give up the right to use or sell the property; it is simply put in another person's name so as to avoid federal estate taxes and probate when you die. The trustee has the power to buy, sell, lease, or invest property according to your instructions, but you have final say as to what happens to all trust property.

Because the trust takes effect while you are still living, it is known as a *revocable* living trust. Revocable means you may end the trust agreement or appoint a different trustee at any time. Property may be added to or taken out of the trust as needed. As grantor, you remain in control of your property. You are merely handing the key to the safe to someone else so that he or she may protect the property within.

Trusts are not a new concept and, in fact, have been around since The Roman Empire, about 800 A.D. Trusts were later used by English knights to help protect their lands when they were called into battle. In America, trusts came into use in the 1700s as a means of helping colonists protect their property from English taxes and government.

Choosing your trustee

You may choose your spouse, a relative, close friend, or knowledgeable financial advisor or attorney to serve as your trustee. The grantor may also serve as his or her own trustee. Although this may seem strange, it is perfectly legal in 49 states; only New York requires you to appoint a co-trustee.

Don't worry if the person(s) you want to name as trustee(s) live in another state or country. Residency in the state where the trust is made is not necessary for selected trustees. However, you may want to be sure that your trustees can be easily contacted. Trustees will need to approve any changes made to the trust.

E-Z TIP

Even if you are your own trustee, your assets are protected from probate, since legally they are owned by the trust, a separate entity, rather than you.

note

No matter who serves as trustee, it is advisable to at least one successor trustee. He/she takes over as trustee if anything prevents the original trustee from performing his/her duties, or upon your death if you are both grantor and trustee.

Many married people name their spouses co-trustees or co-grantors. If you have sufficient confidence in your spouse, you may choose to do this. Both spouses must sign all trust-related documents. However, either spouse as co-grantor, may end the trust without permission from the other.

Upon your death, the trustee automatically distributes the assets in your trust to the people you have designated. These are your beneficiaries, those who receive the property in the trust.

Trustee responsibilities

Trustees must:

- do anything that is directed by the trust agreement

- refrain from doing anything which is forbidden by the trust agreement.

- be familiar with all the terms of the trust

- buy, sell, lease, or invest property according to your trust instructions

note Trustees must deal with the trust property solely for the benefit of the beneficiaries of the trust.

- maintain records and accurate accounts

- act as witnesses to changes to the trust

- act impartially between the beneficiaries of the trust

- protect the assets of the trust

- not delegate the trust powers or duties except when it is sanctioned by the trust or permitted by statute

- transfer the trust property to the persons who are lawfully entitled to receive it

note Trustees are expected to exercise reasonable care in the performance of their duties. In other words, a trustee could conceivably incur liability for negligence. However, the standard of this duty of care can vary between trustees, depending on any special directives. For example, some trustees may be asked to monitor property directly while others may serve as alternative trustees or trust beneficiaries and not have day-to-day control over property matters.

You might ask why you need a trust if you already have a valid will. Won't a will accomplish the same thing?

Better than a will

In fact, a trust is in many cases far superior to a will. Here are nine reasons to establish a living trust:

1)   **You avoid probate.** Most states require individuals with assets of $30,000 or more (or over $10,000 in real estate) to have their estates formally probated when they die. In some states this figure may be as low as $10,000; in other states, only estates with $60,000 or more in assets need go through the probate process.

note
> Unlike a will, where the property remains in your name, a trust takes the property out of your name, allowing you to avoid probate—and its exorbitant costs.

All right, you say, but I don't have anywhere near that much in the bank, so I don't have to worry about it. Wrong. You may not have $30,000 in assets now, but a lot can happen before your death. Inflation tends to drive up property values; so does appreciation. Property worth only $15,000 today may have doubled in value by the time your will is read, putting you over the probate limit. It is smart to plan ahead, and a living trust lets you do just that.

note
With a trust in place your family does not have to go to court, appoint and pay a personal representative to administer your estate, or prove the validity of your intentions. With a trust there are no long delays in distributing

the estate; by contrast, the will probate process can take years, assuming there are no legal complications.

Of course, a will still has its purposes. Parents of minor children may need a will to designate guardianship; people owing or owed money may also have to file a will. However, for most estates, property distribution is much more easily accomplished with a trust.

2)   **You avoid federal estate taxes.** Whether or not you put your assets in a trust, the Economic Recovery Act of 1981 allows for a federal tax exemption (called the Unified Tax Credit Exemption) on all estates. But if you are married, if your estate exceeds this exemption, or if your estate appreciates in value by the time you die, your heirs may face considerable federal estate taxes without the help of a carefully prepared trust.

Your income taxes are unaffected by a living trust. Since the trust is revocable (it only becomes irrevocable upon your death), the I.R.S. does not view it as a permanent entity, and hence does not charge you additional taxes.

> **E-Z TIP**
>
> The goal is to take as much money out of your name as possible, keeping it from the I.R.S. and other agencies so your beneficiaries will inherit it instead.

Because the I.R.S. does not recognize the trust, you do not need a separate tax I.D. number for it. You still pay taxes on the property in the trust, but you would do this anyway. And upon your death, your heirs will save a bundle on federal estate taxes.

3)   **A trust is hard to challenge in court.** One of the worst risks associated with filing a will is that someone may legally challenge its validity in court. It may be someone who has been left out of the will or who received much less than he or she expected. Such court cases are embarrassing, costly and a nuisance you will never have to worry about if you set up a living trust.

Unlike a will, which comes into play after your death, a living trust is administered during your lifetime with your approval, leaving little doubt in anyone's mind that this is how you want your estate to be managed. Hence it is difficult for someone to claim that the trust is a fraud or that you were incompetent when it was formed. And because a trust becomes irrevocable upon your death, no one may interfere with distribution to your intended beneficiaries.

The trust speaks for you, even when you are no longer able to speak for yourself, which gives it more validity than a will.

Some states require you to leave a certain percentage of your property to your spouse regardless of your trust agreement. These states and their laws will be discussed in a following chapter.

A trust may not totally shield you from creditors. Although in some cases a trust may protect your assets in a job-related lawsuit, the protection of a trust is, at best, limited. However, your assets may not be taken if your trustee owes money to creditors; only your debts may be applied to the trust.

4)   **Privacy is assured.** One major disadvantage to probate is that any interested party may see what you left to whom simply by looking up your will at the local probate court. This won't occur with a trust, since the schedule of assets itself does not have to be publicly filed.

5)   **You remain in control of your assets.** A trust guarantees that your beneficiaries are provided for. It also gives you full use of your assets while you are alive, although if there are co-trustees, they both must agree to the disposition of assets. Because of this, it is essential that you appoint someone you know well as a co-trustee if you choose to have a co-trustee.

The appointment of any trustee must be carefully considered. You wouldn't hand over the key to your safe to just anyone; the same holds true for the title to your trust.

While it is wise to appoint someone financially knowledgeable as a trustee (or successor trustee), you must be sure that person will carry out your wishes as you instruct. Many people solve this by appointing one professional trustee—e.g., an accountant or attorney—along with a second trustee who is a close friend or family member and will look out for the grantor's personal interests.

note

Remember, you may make changes to your trust at any time while you are still alive and competent. Trusts may be broken.

Don't feel you are giving up control of your belongings by forming a trust; if anything, you are gaining control by assuring that your assets will go where you want them to.

6) **A trust provides conservatorship rights.** Property is not the only thing a trust protects. You may provide for *conservatorship* through a living trust, meaning you name a person to make your important healthcare decisions and manage your property if you are incapacitated. This very important aspect of a living trust will be detailed in the section on Durable Power of Attorney for Healthcare.

7) **Out-of-state property is protected.** If you own property across state lines, probate is an especially long and difficult process. By contrast, a living trust allows you to administer out-of-state property fairly easily. You may even be able to appoint an out-of-state trustee, or set up your trust in another state so as to take advantage of better tax laws.

8) **Trusts are legally recognized.** Trusts are legally recognized in all 50 states. However, trusts may be regulated differently from state to state, especially in a *community property, dower,* or *curtesy state* where a spouse, by law, is entitled to a part of the estate.

note

Many foreign countries also hold trusts to be valid. Generally, if a country follows British common law, the country will recognize an American-formed trust. If you are considering moving to a foreign country anytime soon, consult an attorney or foreign consulate to determine whether your trust will be upheld.

9)   **The best news of all: trusts are easy.** Living trusts cost little and are easy to form. This is especially true if you research trusts and decide what type you need before you consult an attorney. The point of this book is to help you do just that.

Which type of trust do you need?

Chapter 2

Which type of trust do you need?

What you'll find in this chapter:

⟹ The Unified Tax Credit Exemption advantage

⟹ Maximum estate exemptions

⟹ Providing for your spouse

⟹ About the different types of trusts

⟹ Special considerations for unmarried couples

Trusts can be as varied as individuals. This guide includes a basic single living trust for an individual or married couple whose estate is valued at less than the Unified Tax Credit Exemption (see chart below). If you have assets valued at more than the Exemption, there are two popular trust options to consider: the *A-B Trust* and the *A-B-C Trust*. These are joint trusts for estates exceeding a certain value. You should seek legal advice if you want to set up either of these trusts.

The Unified Tax Credit Exemption

With the the Economic Recovery Act of 1981, $600,000 was the amount established as the maximum value allowed for exemption of one person's estate. A couple could combine this amount, for a total limit of $1.2 million.

As of January 1, 1998, this amount will begin a graduated increase over the next eight years until a maximum of $1 million ($2 million per couple) is reached. You can refer to the following chart to see the amount allowed for exemption each year through 2006:

UNIFIED TAX CREDIT EXEMPTIONS

YEAR	SINGLE	COUPLE	YEAR	SINGLE	COUPLE
pre-1998	$600,000	$1,200,000	2002	$700,000	$1,400,000
1998	$625,000	$1,250,000	2003	$700,000	$1,400,000
1999	$650,000	$1,300,000	2004	$850,000	$1,700,000
2000	$675,000	$1,350,000	2005	$950,000	$1,900,000
2001	$675,000	$1,350,000	2006	$1,000,000	$2,000,000

Dower and curtesy requirements

DEFINITION

A *dower* is the portion of property due the wife by law; a *curtesy* is the property due a husband. Several states have laws requiring grantors to leave a certain amount of money to their spouses. Called dower and curtesy states, they require spouses to leave a minimum of a third to half their property to the surviving spouse. Such laws overrule any contrary conditions set forth in a trust. For example, if you live in a dower state and designate that no more than 10 percent of your property should go to your wife, the state will ignore your wishes and give one-third or more of your property to her.

note The following states are dower and curtesy states: Hawaii, Kentucky, Massachusetts, Michigan, Ohio, Vermont. Consult an attorney if you live in any of these states and plan to set up an A-B or A-B-C Trust.

Community property state guidelines

In community property states, all money earned by a husband and wife during their marriage, and all property bought with that money, is divisible into two equal portions.

In most community property states, if a husband and wife commingle their property—e.g., put all their money in one joint bank account—that property is considered community property. Thus, if either spouse wants an asset not to be considered community property, he

> note
>
> Community property states include: Arizona, California, Idaho, Louisiana, Nevada, New Mexico, Texas, Washington, Wisconsin.

or she must keep it separate (e.g., out of the trust) and legally declare it to be separate property. If you live in a community property state, consider forming two separate trusts, one in your name and the other in your spouse's.

The testamentary trust

Unlike a living trust, the testamentary trust doesn't take effect until after you die. It functions the same way a will does, designating whom you want your property to go to after the first beneficiary. For example, you may designate that your money first goes to your spouse during his or her lifetime, and then the remainder goes to your children as they reach various ages.

The problem with a testamentary trust is that it must go through probate. Unless your total estate is quite small, this is a long, expensive process you want to avoid. Living trusts avoid probate, and for this reason they are generally superior to testamentary trusts. People with estates below the

Unified Tax Credit Exemption may be able to distribute their property using a will and testamentary trust. Most people, however, should consider a living trust.

The insurance trust

Two other popular trusts that you should discuss with your attorney include the insurance trust and the Totten trust. The insurance trust can help couples whose combined estate exceeds the Unified Tax Credit Exemption to divide their estates into two trusts, so that each trust is below the the Unified Tax Credit Exemption limit.

When adding up the value of property in your estate, you are required to include the face value of your life insurance. Couples with substantial insurance may find their total estate value exceeds the Unified Tax Credit Exemption cutoff for untaxed inheritances, forcing them to pay those dreaded estate taxes. Putting the insurance into a separate trust deducts the face value from your estate, giving you fewer assets in the eyes of the government and allowing you to meet tax limits.

There are a few points to consider before setting up an insurance trust. First, it is irrevocable. This means that once you put your insurance funds into the trust, you cannot get that money back, even if you need it later. You may, however, still change insurance companies. Second, your beneficiaries must pay premiums on the insurance policy.

If you die within three years of forming the insurance trust, your family will still face an estate tax. Therefore, set up an insurance trust only if you are physically and financially healthy enough to accept the risks involved. Those with estates over the Unified Tax Credit Exemption limit and with large insurance policies will benefit most.

DEFINITION

Many people whose primary assets are bank funds utilize a so-called *Totten trust*, where a trustee (often the grantor) manages a bank account while he or she is living and the account funds go to a named beneficiary upon the grantor's death—without probate.

The irrevocable living trust

Property assigned to the irrevocable living trust is exempt from federal estate taxes because the trust is not considered to be part of the grantor's taxable estate. However, an irrevocable trust may not be changed or revoked once it has been established. A trust is irrevocable unless it contains a statement specifically saying it can be revoked. Control may only be established thorough detailed descriptions in the trust document itself, of management and beneficiaries.

CAUTION Never establish an irrevocable trust without first obtaining qualified legal advice. Giving up the right to control and amend your trust should never be taken lightly.

The spendthrift trust

Another specialized trust is the spendthrift trust. This trust is designed to protect the assets of the trust from the creditors of the beneficiary's reckless spending. Typically, the beneficiary's creditors cannot reach the principal and interest of the trust until it is received by the beneficiary. The beneficiary may not assign the principal and interest before receiving it. This effectively prevents a beneficiary, who is in a hurry to receive his inheritance, from selling his interest to another—often at a discount—before the estate is settled.

Types of trusts

There are many different types of trusts. Choose the trust that is best for your needs:

- **A Trust:** for singles or couples with less than UTCE

- **A-B Trust:** for couples

- **A-B-C Trust:** for couples with assets over the UTCE or w/children from previous marriages

- **Testamentary Trust:** goes into effect after grantor dies

- **Insurance Trust:** special trust to hold insurance policies or proceeds

> *note* Totten trusts, also called pay-on-death (POD) accounts, are most often used as a means to avoid probate for bank accounts, government bonds, individual retirement accounts and, possibly, securities or a car.

- **Totten or Pay-on-death Trust:** bank account trust

- **Revocable Trust:** a general term meaning a trust can be revoked at any time prior to the grantor's death.

- **Pour-Over-Will Trust:** supplement to the trust

Unmarried couples

Unmarried couples reading this section are probably wondering: How about us? Do we have the legal right to form trusts and enjoy these tax savings as married couples do?

The answer is yes—and no. Unmarried couples do have equal rights in most states when it comes to forming a trust. However, many community property states do not allow you the same estate tax benefits as married couples. Unmarried couples would therefore do well to consult an attorney knowledgeable about trusts to see what their specific state laws are at this time.

note

As public views change toward unwed unions, trust laws are likely to change as well. Even now the laws regarding single couples and trusts are much more liberal than in the past.

Getting it together

Chapter 3
Getting it together

What you'll find in this chapter:

➠ What to prepare before you see an attorney

➠ Successor trustees and beneficiaries

➠ Scheduling your assets

➠ How to transfer property and assets to a trust

➠ How to file trust documents

Now that you've decided which trust is right for you, your next step is to see an attorney, right? Wrong. Most attorneys charge by the hour; if you don't have all your documents together and know where you're headed before you walk through the law office door, you'll waste time and money discussing things you can handle on your own. You will need a lawyer at some point, but not just yet.

Your main business at this point is to do what the title of this chapter implies: get your legal documents together, along with the forms you must file with the appropriate agencies. You will need to draw up a *Schedule of Assets* and locate any real estate deeds, corporate stock certificates, bank books and other proof of property ownership in preparation for transferring your assets to a trust.

Talk to your family

Before you gather anything together, speak to your family about the trust. This may seem obvious, yet it is often overlooked. Most likely your family members will be your designated beneficiaries. Someone from your family may also serve as co-trustee or successor trustee. If your children are worried about their financial futures, they will be reassured to learn that a trust will provide for them in the best way possible. They should also know where to find your important financial documents when you are no longer living. Questions you and your family must decide include:

◆ *Who should serve as the successor trustees (assuming you are the trustee during your lifetime)?*

You will need to choose up to three people to fill the successor trustee roles. Find people you and your family feel comfortable with to look out for your interests. An adult child with sound judgment may serve as a successor trustee. At least one of your successor trustees should have

> *note* Amending your trust requires the approval of all co-trustees, so select trustees and successor trustees who can be available for this responsibility on an on-going basis.

basic legal/accounting knowledge, as he or she must submit complicated tax forms. Often a stipend is provided to the successor trustee in return for these duties.

◆ *Who will be your beneficiaries and contingent beneficiaries?*

In most cases, your spouse and children will be your main beneficiaries. However, you need to consider who your money will go to if you should outlive any of your main beneficiaries. These second-choice beneficiaries are contingent beneficiaries of the trust.

Often when considering beneficiaries, people forget about giving to charity. Most contributions are tax deductible—an added bonus—but they are also a wonderful way to thank an organization that has helped you or your family. Perhaps there is a college, hospital, or other nonprofit institution you would like to help with a specified donation from your estate. Often these institutions have Planned Giving Officers whose job is to help people set up charitable bequests. If this type of giving is of interest to you, contact the organization in question and request to speak to the Planned Giving Officer or someone else on the fundraising staff.

◆ *What are the needs of each beneficiary, and how will the trust provide for him or her?*

If you are the parent of young children, put a clause in your trust designating money for a college education. Perhaps you have a family member who will require caretaking when you are no longer around. Who will do that, and how much will it cost?

The trick here is to try to project 20 to 30 years ahead, a seemingly impossible task since some situations are likely to change. Marriages occur or fail. Families grow. Health deteriorates. Remember, too, that costs are likely to double every ten years or so due to inflation. A good tool to help you look into your financial future is E-Z Legal Software's *Financial Forecaster* program.

note
A lawyer or accountant may be able to help you project costs, but only you know your family's needs.

Be as specific as possible when setting up your trust. If you put in a clause about your child's education, for example, you may define the word "education" so that a successor trustee understands what is and is not covered. If your child chooses a technical school instead of a college, is that to be paid for by the trust? Will the trust pay for graduate school?

Review with your successor trustees what their duties will be. Make sure they are willing and able to take on a considerable amount of responsibility. Also settle how much they will be paid (if at all) for their help so there is no misunderstanding later, and put this amount in writing.

Next, a Schedule of Assets

To draw up a list of the assets in your estate, number each asset and give a detailed description of its appearance, function, location, and type of ownership (for example, whether you own it separately or if it is jointly owned with your spouse). Write down your estimate of its fair market value (replacement cost). You may need to have some items appraised by a professional if there is doubt as to their present worth. Make sure to include the face value of all existing life insurance policies in your asset total.

A lawyer or accountant can look over the list later for accuracy; at this point you simply want a working total on which to base your initial decision-making. Add your total assets together. Next, figure out your debts, including mortgages, bank loans, and other expenses. Again, you are merely looking for an approximate figure—it doesn't have to be exact.

Subtract your debts from your assets to get the net worth of your estate. This will give you an idea of how much in estate taxes your family will have to pay, as well as the total value of the assets that will go into the trust. This list you have just drawn up is called a Schedule of Assets. It will be attached to your trust agreement and serve as proof that you intended to include these assets as part of your trust. It also provides your family and successor trustees with a map of where to find each asset.

note Do include in your living trust any motor vehicle such as an antique or classic car purchased as an investment or on which you spent considerable money restoring.

There are several assets that should not be included in a trust. Checking accounts worth less than $30,000 are best left out, since they are not subject to probate and your spouse automatically inherits them. Also leave out personally owned motor vehicles, as these tend to depreciate in value and will not be probated either, and do not include either insurance not payable to the estate or subchapter S corporate stock.

Check with your local county tax assessor before transferring your primary residence to a revocable living trust. The transfer may be viewed as a change in ownership, triggering the "due-on-sale" clause and jeopardizing the homestead exemption.

Most assets will go into the trust, especially if there is any chance they will bring your estate total over the probate limit.

The following items are included on a typical Schedule of Assets:

- safe deposit boxes

- real estate

- stocks (excluding S Corporation stock)

- bonds

- accounts receivable

- businesses (solely owned, partnerships, corporate interests)

- bank accounts over $30,000

- household furniture

> *note* Remember, an exempt homestead may also include a mobile home or a boat. Check with your county tax assessor.

- jewelry

- life insurance payable to the estate

- mutual funds

- mortgages/liens

- miscellaneous personal property

- intangible items (e.g., copyrights, trademarks and patents)

In some cases a married couple will transfer one partner's retirement benefits into the trust as well. This is not always advisable; consult an attorney. If you transfer an employer-paid pension, speak to your company's personnel officer about what benefits will be coming to you upon your retirement; have the benefits go to your spouse as first beneficiary, followed by the trust as a contingent beneficiary. That way if your spouse is no longer living at the time benefits become payable, the benefits will automatically go to the trust without probate.

Once you have decided what you will put in your trust, you need to gather all documents related to those items. Find your deed, insurance policies, stock certificates, mortgage documents, and anything else that proves property ownership. Jointly owned property may be transferred into the trust with the approval of your spouse, so there should not be any problem if an item is in both spouses' names.

note Persons intending to receive Medicaid may be required to file for Medicaid at least two years before setting up a trust. Check with your attorney if this is an issue.

Transferring property to a trust

Simply listing your assets on the schedule of assets does not transfer them to the trust. To do this, the trust must obtain title to those assets.

Helpful tips on how to transfer your different assets to a trust is found later in this chapter. Usually the total transfer process takes several weeks, depending upon how much property you have. You may want to transfer assets in stages or steps. A thoughtful plan written down in advance of starting your trust can help you pace this effort.

> **E-Z TIP**
> Make copies of the blank Assignment of Property form before you fill it in so you will have extras for any future changes.

First, list each item of personal property to be put in trust on the *Assignment of Property to Trust* form. It is important to include everything of value in the trust.

Financial officers at your bank will help you transfer any bank account funds to a special trust account. They may ask to see part of your trust agreement. While there, arrange to rent a safe deposit box in which to keep some of your assets. (Maintaining trust assets will be discussed later.)

> **CAUTION** Always use your full legal name on all documents; otherwise their validity may be challenged.

Your bank will keep a *signature card* on file showing that a trust account exists; be certain when you sign trust checks that your signature is on behalf of the trust. Also specify to bank officials whether one trustee alone may sign on behalf of the trust regarding bank transactions or whether all trustees need to sign. If you don't specify this, the bank may require all parties to sign all documents.

Some assets may only be transferred by obtaining the signatures of third parties. Stock transfers may require a call or visit to your broker, as the stock certificates must be changed to reflect that the trust is the new owner. A small securities transfer tax may be charged.

The *Schedule of Assets* and *Assignment of Property* forms are attached to the main trust document, known as the revocable living trust. Essentially this document lists the grantors, trustees/successor trustees, trust property, beneficiaries, how the

> **E-Z TIP**
>
> Never commingle funds, or mix funds from outside the trust with funds from within the trust. Maintain two checking accounts—one for the trust and another for your own personal needs.

property is to be divided, and the state whose laws will govern the trust (usually your state of residence). It also contains any special conditions that may apply—e.g., at what age your children should receive their inheritances, or even provisions for taking care of your pets. Name and date your trust. Trusts are commonly named after the grantor making the trust. For example, if your name is John Smith, you may name your trust *The John Smith Trust*, or the *Smith Family Trust*. Insert the name of your trust on the top of your revocable living trust, after "Known as."

note

Check your state laws if you are disinheriting a spouse or child from receiving property, because not all states allow you to do so. It is advisable to attach to the trust a separate note of instructions stating why you are disinheriting. Otherwise the disinherited person may take the estate to court after your death, and might successfully challenge your trust. Giving your attorney a note with the reasons for the disinheritance is an option in place of attaching the note to the trust.

A third document, the *Certificate of Trustees' Powers,* is also commonly attached to the trust document. The Certificate shows which powers you are giving your successor trustee, such as the right to sell, buy, or lease your property.

Signing your trust

Execute your revocable living trust as you would a will. The trust must be signed by the grantor, in the presence of three witnesses. The three witnesses must sign in the grantor's presence and in the presence of each other.

Filing trust documents

The *Certificate of Trustees' Powers* often gets filed publicly in place of the revocable living trust, which is advantageous because although it lists the trustees and beneficiaries, it does not show who inherits how much. You should also file an *Affidavit of Succession*. This states the terms for changing trustees if your present or successor trustees become mentally incompetent or otherwise unable to serve.

DEFINITION

Several states have adopted the *Uniform Probate Code*. This Code requires you, the grantor, to publicly file your trust with the county recorder. Check with your local Probate Registry to see if this applies to your state and the specific filing procedures you must pursue.

Even if your state does not require you to record your trust, you should consider doing so. Recording it offers legal proof that the trust exists, and shows that you intended to distribute your property according to the trust agreement. Before you file anything publicly, bring the documents to a trust attorney to ensure that you have filled them out right.

Once all papers are signed, make copies for your trustees, attorney, accountant, beneficiaries, and others who need to have information on your financial arrangements. Keep a copy in your home or safe deposit box for easy reference.

Finally, make sure you keep one or more assets in your trust at all times. A trust with no assets legally transferred to it is considered invalid. You must put at least one asset into the trust before it will take effect, so make sure the Transfer Forms and Deeds are filled out properly.

> *note*
>
> All trusts must be notarized. Bring three witnesses and your trustees to the Notary Public's office, along with the trust documents.

Now take a deep breath and relax. You have just covered the major steps for setting up a living trust.

This doesn't mean you are finished, however. Later, you will learn how to maintain your living trust from year to year as changes occur. There are also additional documents to include those things your trust can't handle or that you want to keep separate.

How to transfer assets to your trust

Business Transfers — Use the Assignment of Property to Trust form in the back of this guide for solely owned businesses; for partnerships, get written permission from each partner and fill out the Assignment of Property form.

Corporate Stock — Fill out the assignment on the back of the stock certificate; sign it and mark "Canceled" on the back; have a new certificate issued for the same amount of shares in the trust's name.

Deeds of Trust (When someone owes you money and pledges their real estate) — In addition to including the promissory note on the Assignment of Property form, have your attorney draw up a special Assignment of Property form for the real estate that's involved.

Follow-up to ensure that the Assignment of Property form is recorded with the county recorder's office in the name of your trust. That helps ensure that the property may not be sold until the debtor has repaid the money they owe you.

Insurance Policies — Call your life insurance firm and request a Change of Beneficiary form; list your trust as the beneficiary; send the form back.

Be careful to transfer only the beneficial interest of your assets, not ownership, for such things as your IRA, pension plan, stock and bonds, insurance and annuities.

Intangible Items (such as copyrights and patents) — Include each item on the Assignment of Property form; give notice to the U.S. Patent or Copyright Office.

Motor Vehicles (Do not transfer unless so advised by an attorney) — Include on the *Assignment of Property* form; go to the nearest Registry of Motor Vehicles and fill out an official Endorsement of Ownership Certificate transferring the motor vehicle to the name of the trust.

Personal Items — Include each item on the Assignment of Property to Trust form.

Promissory Notes — Endorse the front of the note in the name of the trust; fill out a Transfer form.

Real Estate — Have your attorney make out a new deed with the trust as the owner; file the deed with the local Registry of Deeds, along with the Certificate of Trustees' Powers, showing your trustee's power to buy and sell the property. There is usually a small recording fee involved in this process; call your local registry or county recorder's office for the amount. If a mortgage is involved, you must speak with the lending company about transferring title.

Check with your county tax assessor before transferring your primary residence to a revocable living trust. If your county views such as transfer as a change in ownership, you may lose your homestead exemption, trigger the "due on sale" clause in your mortgage, and give rise to a new assessment.

> *note* If you decide to refinance in the future, your real estate will have to be taken out of the trust, but may be returned to the trust immediately afterward.

Retirement Benefits — Consult your attorney.

Safe Deposit Box — These may not legally be put in the name of the trust; they must be in the name of an individual. Transfer items in the safe deposit box to the trust instead, by including them on the Assignment of Property to Trust form; ask a bank officer if you have questions.

Savings Accounts, Certificates of Deposit and Treasury Bills — Show a copy of your trust agreement to the bank officer; fill out a signature card indicating who needs to sign trust documents; have these accounts put in the name of the trust.

You can transfer your checking account(s) to your trust, and still leave your name and address on the checks. By not putting the name of the trust on the checks, you help to avoid any confusion when you go to write a check.

Stocks and Bonds — Obtain a Stock Power form from your broker; turn over old stock and a copy of your trust agreement; have stock and bonds reissued in the name of the trust. (Series EE Bonds may be transferred by going to your nearest Federal Reserve Bank; bring a copy of your trust agreement.)

Stocks and bonds are nonnegotiable until they are signed. Once signed, anyone can negotiate the stocks and bonds! For added protection, forward the unsigned stocks or bonds and the Stock Power form in separate envelopes. When both are received, they can then be put together and negotiated.

Estate planning basics

4

Chapter 4

Estate planning basics

What you'll find in this chapter:

➡ Estate planning basics

➡ The pour-over will

➡ Naming your guardians and caregivers

➡ Duties of your guardians and caregivers

➡ Your estate plan checklist

While a trust will cover the monetary distribution, it does not deal with the more personal aspects of your estate—e.g., who will care for your minor children if something happens to you, or who will make decisions for you if you lose your mental competency. Such issues are usually best left to the documents discussed in this chapter.

The pour-over will

For starters, what if you leave an asset out of your trust? Very few trust grantors have perfect memories. Many become careless over the years and forget to add items to their trusts, which is why the catch-all pour-over will was created. Unlike the standard will, which replaces a trust, the pour-over will is designed to supplement a trust by protecting those assets you should have included in the trust but didn't. Pour-over wills state that all assets left out

DEFINITION

---

of the trust that should have been included are to be included in the trust at that time.

To provide a pour-over provision for your trust, simply add the following provision to your will:

"The remainder of my estate wherever located, I give to the trustee or trustees named under a certain Revocable Living Trust executed on January 1, 1995, between myself and the trustee of AnyTrust in the county of AnyCounty and State of AnyState, to be added to the principal of the trust and to be administered in all respects as an integral part of that trust."

> **note**
> Remember, assets covered by this pour-over provision are subject to probate, so it is best to review your trust regularly to ensure all your assets are safely listed in your trust.

Naming guardians

An updated will does more than protect your money—it protects your family's personal interests. Besides putting stray assets back into your trust using a pour-over clause, a will may be used to designate guardians for minor or disabled adult children. Speak to an attorney to see if such a will is appropriate in your case. Read Last Wills & Testament Made E-Z. It contains all the forms and instructions needed to complete your own will.

> **E-Z TIP**
> Be specific when naming children's legal guardians and the custody rights they will have. For example, if you want your sister to have custody of your children, but you are concerned that she and her husband may separate, clearly state that custody goes only to your sister and not to her estranged husband.

Speak to those you are naming guardians before you name them in the will. Appoint people you have known for a long time; if possible, choose close family members. Make sure the people you choose for such major roles understand—and want—their assigned duties.

The duties of the guardian include:

- to possess and manage the minor's property

- to manage and invest the minor's assets

- to use the funds for the benefit of the minor

- to provide a regular accounting to the probate court

- to file and pay the minor's taxes

- to distribute the remaining funds to the minor when he or she reaches adulthood

note
In addition to being responsible for providing care, comfort and education for the child, the guardian is also responsible for the child's property. Therefore, if you are leaving property to a minor, that property must be entrusted to the guardian.

While you are considering the finances that will be necessary to support the child, if it is within your means to do so, consider compensating the guardian. The guardian is going to be asked to post a bond with the court. While this bond is an expression of good faith, you may state in your will that the guardian is to serve without posting bond.

If you have any doubts, choose alternate guardians instead. Your children are not the only ones who may need guardians.

note
As people live longer, more and more are reaching an age where their mental capacities decline and physical problems arise. When people are unable to care for themselves, their families must go through a public,

humiliating process to gain conservatorship over them and their estates. This is another area in which a good estate plan can help.

Naming caregivers

Several documents deal specifically with the issues of healthcare and conservatorship. The Durable General Power of Attorney allows a competent adult to make decisions for you if you are unable to speak for yourself.

DEFINITION

Before Durable Powers of Attorney, the only option was to have the court appoint a *conservator* (a court-appointed custodian of property belonging to a person determined to be unable to properly manage his property). This is not always a desirable alternative for three reasons:

1)   ***The time delay.*** It may take several weeks or even months to have a conservator appointed who will have the authority to make medical decisions for you. With a durable power of attorney your agent can act for you immediately. You thus avoid the vulnerability that comes when you lack the continuous ability to protect your interests.

2)   ***Selection of Agent.*** When you are ill or disabled you lose the ability to select your conservator or guardian. The court may or may not appoint the conservator who you prefer. Moreover, you may decide upon one person to make health care decisions for you and select another to manage your financial or business affairs. This is only possible when you appoint these individuals while you have the capacity to act.

3)   ***Cost.*** The process of having a conservator appointed by a court could be costly. The fees can range from hundreds to thousands of dollars depending upon the state you live in, the complexity of the case and whether it is a contested proceeding. These costs are eliminated when you designate your own agent.

This is especially important if you have property that needs to be added to the trust and you are unable to do it. While a revocable living trust agreement gives your successor trustee the right to manage property inside the trust after your death and your will gives your appointed executor the right to manage outside assets after your death or upon your incapacitation, neither document protects assets outside the trust if you are living but mentally impaired. The Durable General Power of Attorney provides this coverage, allowing an appointed person to take over automatically without conservatorship proceedings.

A separate document, the Durable Power of Attorney for Healthcare, deals specifically with healthcare decision-making. As with the General Power of Attorney, it takes effect only if you are unable to make your own decisions; however, it must be drawn up *while you are still competent* or it will be declared invalid. That is why it is important to draw up an estate plan now.

A Durable Power of Attorney for Healthcare states whether you give a hospital permission to use artificial means to save or prolong your life—increasingly an issue as medical technology improves. In many states if you do not designate what you want done, the attending physician has no choice but to use artificial life support systems, even if your family objects. However, if you put in writing what you do and do not want, and if you appoint someone to speak on your behalf, your wishes will almost always be upheld.

Name a trustworthy individual as your decisionmaker in a Power of Attorney for Healthcare. This person will have access to your medical records. Make sure he or she agrees with your view on such issues as artificial life support, and that your wishes will be carried out.

> *note*
> You may want to file a Directive to Physicians, also called a Living Will, which deals specifically with the life support issue and leaves no room for doubt on this matter. You will still need to file a Power of Attorney for Healthcare to cover other health-related matters.

DEFINITION A clause within the revocable living trust also allows you to select a *conservator,* the person you want to care for you physically on an everyday basis in the event you are unable to care for yourself. Again, it is important to choose the right person; think through your decision carefully.

There are some protections you should take in filing the above healthcare-related documents. First, put a clause in your Power of Attorney for Healthcare giving you the right to appoint a new conservator if you should change your mind. This protects you if your first-choice conservator doesn't work out for any reason.

Second, put in a clause stating at what point you may be ruled incompetent. The best policy is to require at least two physicians to agree on your incompetence before the Power of Attorney goes into effect.

Third, all of the above documents must be witnessed by at least three people, none of whom may be your relatives, healthcare providers, conservator, personal representative, guardian, or beneficiary. Documents should be notarized and sent to all of your regular healthcare providers so they will have copies if and when the documents go into effect.

Your estate plan should now include the following:

- Revocable Living Trust with conservator nomination

- Schedule of Assets

- Schedule of Beneficiaries

- Certificate of Trustees' Powers

- Amendment to Trust

- Revocation of Trust

- Affidavit of Succession

- Assignment of Property to Trust

- Bill of Sale

The above forms are found in this guide. Your living trust should also have the following:

- Deed showing transfer of real estate to the trust

- Stock certificates made out to the trust

- Life insurance policies naming trust as beneficiary

- Checkbooks in the trust's name (if funds exceed probate limit)

- Last Will & Testament with pour-over provision

- Durable General Power of Attorney

- Durable Power of Attorney for Healthcare

- Directive to Physicians

Flip through the forms and instructions now to get a feel for what you will be filling out. Several forms used to amend and terminate trust agreements are also included in this guide and are discussed later.

When you need expert advice

5

Chapter 5

When you need expert advice

What you'll find in this chapter:

➧ The $600,000+ exemption

➧ Tax questions and the living trust

➧ How to decide if you need expert advice

➧ Questions to ask an attorney

➧ Should you have a will?

You will save time—and possibly money—by reading this guide and getting to know your financial options. However, there are several reasons why you should see an attorney about your trust.

> **note**
> The point of this guide is not to help you avoid attorneys and their associated costs. Attorneys have extensive training that no guide is going to teach you in a few chapters.

First, local and federal estate laws are constantly changing. As stated earlier, wills made before 1981 should be amended because of the 1981 Economic Recovery Act, which gave every person the $600,000 exemption. This exemption now increases each year to a maximum $675,000 in the year 2001. This is one good reason to

see an attorney: if the laws change, attorneys are usually the first to know and can help organize your estate accordingly.

UNIFIED TAX CREDIT EXEMPTIONS

Year	Single	Couple
pre-1998	$600,000	$1,200,000
1998	$625,000	$1,250,000
1999	$650,000	$1,300,000
2000	$675,000	$1,350,000
2001	$675,000	$1,350,000
2002	$700,000	$1,400,000
2003	$700,000	$1,400,000
2004	$850,000	$1,700,000
2005	$950,000	$1,900,000
2006	$1,000,000	$2,000,000

In the event your gross estate as grantor exceeds the Unified Tax Credit Exemption, individually or combined, you may minimize your estate taxes by having you and your spouse set up separate reciprocal living trusts often called "credit shelter trusts" or "A-B trusts." This estate planning tool allows your estate to pass to the trust rather than directly to the surviving spouse. The trust, in turn, provides the surviving spouse with a lifetime income. Since your trustee must be aware of your intention to use this trust, you may provide the following sample instructions:

"If my spouse shall survive me, I direct that my entire trust estate be given to my trustee(s) to be divided into two separate trusts which are herein referred to as "Trust A" and "Trust B."

a) Trust A shall have placed into it the sum of $_____. Said sum represents one-half of the value of my adjusted gross estate as defined by the Internal Revenue code for the purposes of the marital deduction. Trust A shall be reduced *to the extent allowed under the Internal Revenue Code, by the value of all assets that pass or have passed to my spouse other than by the terms of this paragraph and that satisfy the marital deduction.*

b) Trust B shall have placed into it an amount equal to the balance of my residuary estate after deducting the amount allocated to Trust A."

Other tax questions

Generally, a living trust poses no special tax problems. Here, however, are some pointers on the most commonly asked questions:

- ***Is there a taxable consequence when property is transferred into the trust?***

No. however, the transfer of securities to or from a living trust may incur a securities transfer tax in some states. If you plan to transfer substantial amounts of stock, check first with your accountant or attorney.

- ***Is it necessary for the trust to file its own tax return?***

There is no need to get a separate taxpayer identification number for the trust or file a fiduciary income tax return as long as you appoint yourself or your spouse as trustee.

- ***What tax problems arise if the trust is set up in a state other than where the grantor resides?***

There is a possibility of double state income taxation should you set up a living trust in another state. This problem can be resolved by setting up the trust in the state where you reside. Should you move to another state, you can amend the living trust to reflect that it will be governed by the laws of your new state.

- ***Does a living trust affect personal income taxes?***

A living trust does not change your personal income tax obligation. Even when income (i.e., a personal paycheck) is deposited directly into the trust, you must still report and pay taxes on the income. Similarly, you can deduct tax-deductible expenses, notwithstanding their payment from the trust.

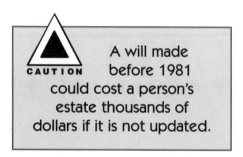

A will made before 1981 could cost a person's estate thousands of dollars if it is not updated.

Those who have estates worth more than the Unified Tax Credit Exemption may need to set up more complicated trusts if they are to keep their money away from tax collectors. Those with nontraditional family situations—pending divorces, stepchildren, adult children who need conservatorship—must set up their trusts carefully to make sure their money goes where it should. A qualified attorney can give you further information on specialized trusts, such as insurance trusts and spendthrift trusts, if you ask (and by using this guide you will know what to ask).

When to ask an attorney

Persons who are in the following situations should always seek an attorney's advice:

- Those who live in community property, dower or curtesy states (particularly if you do not want to leave half of your property to your spouse, you are not naming your spouse as co-trustee, or you are seeking a divorce)

- Non-U.S. citizens (there are limits on your ability to participate in a trust agreement)

- Those receiving veterans' benefits or applying for Medicaid (these may sometimes be affected by estate planning)

 You should not seek trust advice from an attorney whose main area of practice is litigation or criminal law. If your regular attorney has no trust experience, look for someone else to handle this aspect of your legal affairs.

Questions to ask an attorney

What questions should you ask when shopping around? Try the following:

◆ *How many trusts have you handled in the last five years?*

You want someone who is up to date on regulations. If you are an attorney's first trust client, or even the second, you'll probably want to shop further.

Attorney fees can be much higher for living trusts than for those charged to draft a will. You may be able to lower those fees considerably with good advance planning and by completing documents that help you toward the final package.

◆ *Have you handled clients with estates the size of mine?*

This is important if you are one of those people in the million-dollar range. Some attorneys may only have handled smaller estates; this does not mean you can't use such a person—it's just something for you to keep in mind.

◆ *Will you handle my case personally?*

This question is appropriate for attorneys at larger law firms. You may be paying a big name to handle your estate, but in fact most of the actual legal work might be done by associate attorneys or, increasingly, by the firm's paralegals. While it is all right for assistants to submit forms and handle lesser matters, make sure the attorney you are paying will be available when needed.

◆ *How much do you charge?*

This is, of course, the big question. It is also an area where you may well receive an incomplete reply. Once the attorney gives you an amount, follow up with:

◆ *What services does the amount you just quoted include?*

You ask this question because some attorneys may quote you a partial price. Perhaps the fee includes your initial consultation and one or two follow-up visits, but not the documents your attorney will "discover" must be filed during those visits. Some attorneys charge fixed rates; other attorneys work by the hour. Ask about "hidden" fees, such as photocopying, postage, and typing expenses. Most attorneys are fair, but

> **E-Z TIP**
> Many people claim to be financial advisors. Some have adequate credentials; others don't. If you choose a financial planner over an accountant, ask for proof of certification to make sure the planner is properly trained.

there are those who will charge for anything they can get away with. Expect to pay a retainer fee; also expect the cost to be higher if you are setting up a specialized trust arrangement—e.g., an insurance trust or A-B-C trust for a large estate.

 Ask family, friends, and neighbors with trusts who they recommend. You may also be able to get the name of a competent attorney from your bank.

note Let your attorney know that you want to make informed decisions, especially in terms of planning for your family's financial future. A knowledgeable attorney will welcome a client who already knows something about trusts, as it will save him or her a lot of time having to explain the basics.

Some banks have their own trust departments, with advisors who will review your financial situation and make recommendations. (Usually there is a small charge for this.) They may be able to look over the net worth estimates you have prepared for your estate, along with your Schedule of Assets, and tell if your planning is headed in the right direction.

If your bank does not offer such services, you may choose to meet with an accountant instead. Do this before you see an attorney. Have the accountant work with you to prepare your net worth statement and Schedule of Assets. This is the best way to ensure that these things get done right.

Again, get all your documents together and discuss things with your family before you see an attorney. Make copies of the forms in this book and fill them out the way you intend to fill out the final versions. You can show these to your attorney and have any mistakes corrected.

note The main thing an attorney will do is fit your trust to meet your needs. The forms in this guide contain generalized language which, in most situations, will be enough to protect your estate. However, there may be certain clauses specific to your property that should be included as well. An attorney will translate these clauses into legalese and add them to the general forms.

Your attorney should review every trust document before you sign. Don't expect to finish things in one or two visits. You may well need one or more initial consultations, after which you may be called back to sign the final documents. Even the least complicated trusts normally take one to two months to get filed.

Should you have a will?

Some attorneys may recommend a will instead of a trust. Wills and probate are very attractive to attorneys because of the fees involved. Numerous documents must be drawn up as part of the probate process. Relatives must be notified and must return legal forms to the attorney's office; military affidavits must be filed; notices to creditors must be published in newspapers; there are complicated estate tax forms to deal with, all of which earn the attorney fees.

> **E-Z Tip**
>
> Those who benefit most from having a will are single persons with smaller estates and no legal dependents. If this describes you and your attorney recommends a will instead, consider it. Otherwise, a trust probably makes more sense for you financially.

Attorneys usually earn far less for helping a client form a trust, as a trust may be administered largely without legal assistance. Examine the cost of a trust vs. a will, and then ask for the what specific advantages you gain by preparing a will.

It's your trust

Also keep in mind that you are the one who best knows your family's needs. If an attorney tries to push you into doing something that makes you uncomfortable—a financial arrangement that will affect your children's futures in a major way, for example—don't hesitate to get a second opinion.

 Check with your attorney from time to time regarding changes in trust regulations that could affect your estate. Do not depend on your attorney to get in touch with you. Often lawyers have many more clients than they are able to keep track of, so the communication process will be your responsibility.

Married couples should note that in some cases the government will reward your financial planning efforts with a special tax break. (Unfortunately this does not yet apply to single persons.) Ask your attorney for a signed receipt showing that you have put together an A-B or A-B-C trust. If a professional does your tax forms for you, ask that the tax break be noted directly on the tax form. If you do the form yourself, write a note and put it in with your other tax documents so

Make copies of all forms you sign. Put the signed original in a safe place to ensure that you don't lose it and to protect it from natural disasters.

that when it is time to file taxes you'll remember to list your trust in the deduction section and take off money accordingly. That alone makes forming a trust worth the effort.

Making changes

Chapter 6
Making changes

What you'll find in this chapter:

➡ Changing your trust

➡ Record-keeping essentials

➡ The trust notebook

➡ Changing trustees

➡ How to dissolve your trust

Forming your revocable living trust takes only a month or two; maintaining it is a lifelong—but easy—process. It is important to know the status of your trust at all times and to make changes as necessary.

The responsibility for trust maintenance falls to you, the grantor, and your co-trustees. Once a year review any changes that may have occurred. Just as you would not store your possessions in a safe without unlocking it and taking a peek inside every now and then, you should not neglect the assets in your trust.

note Your successor trustees should ask any questions they have about the trust now, while you are still living. This will avoid unnecessary confusion later.

Keeping scrupulous records

One of the most important duties of a trustee is to maintain accurate, up-to-date financial records. The grantor plays a role in this. If you purchase an item after the trust has been formed and want to add that item to the trust, list the trust as owner on the bill of sale. This is how any personal items will be added to the trust. In addition, you must list each asset you purchase on your Schedule of Assets, giving a full description of the item and its location.

If you buy stock after the trust is formed, put the trust's name on the certificates. Real estate deeds for any property you purchase also need to be owned by the trust.

If you sell a trust asset, this modification should be noted as well. Fill out an Assignment of Property form for each item you sell, listing the trust as the seller and transferring title to the new owner. Keep the receipts from all trust asset sales. Also officially

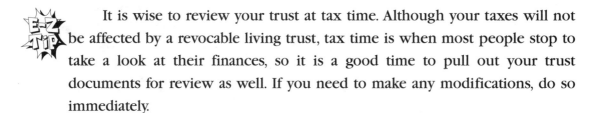

CAUTION Do not leave anything of value out of your trust. Remember, if you leave it out, your estate may be subject to probate.

delete the item from your Schedule of Assets and note the date, so that your successor trustee does not think the item is still part of the trust. You have to be scrupulous about your record keeping. If you add to or sell something from your estate, don't put off noting the change in your records.

It is wise to review your trust at tax time. Although your taxes will not be affected by a revocable living trust, tax time is when most people stop to take a look at their finances, so it is a good time to pull out your trust documents for review as well. If you need to make any modifications, do so immediately.

The trust notebook

Many people find it handy to set up a trust notebook. This is a loose-leaf binder in which you put copies of all trust-related documents so that they are all in one place.

Divide your trust notebook into three sections: Legal Documents, Bills of Sale, and Letters of Instruction. The first section, *Legal Documents*, should contain the revocable living trust, Certificate of Trustees' Powers, Schedule of Assets, and Assignment of Property to Trust forms. It should also include any amendments used to modify the trust, as will be discussed later in this chapter.

The *Bills of Sale* section contains proof of ownership for those items purchased after the original trust agreement was formed. Bills of Sale for newly purchased items and receipts for those assets you sell will go here. Copies of deeds, stock certificates, and insurance policies should go here as well. (The originals of these items should be placed in your safe deposit box.)

The third section, *Letters of Instruction*, contains your letter to your successor trustee, telling him or her who to contact about specific trust assets when you die. Your trustee need not notify any probate court or federal agency upon your death. However, the trustee must contact your stock broker, mortgage company, and insurance company about transferring or selling your assets, or to handle some other matters. Your Letter of Instruction provides a handy framework for the trustee during this process.

note Remember: You don't have to put everything you own into a trust, especially if you are concerned about maintaining all the records.

Often your attorney can draw up such a letter for you. You may also leave a letter requesting that your successor trustee call your attorney and get full instructions on what to do upon your death.

Consider keeping some things out of the trust, for example the car you drive and other personal property, to cut down on record-keeping. Then, use a will to bequeath all assets not in your trust.

Healthcare-related documents also go in the third section of your trust notebook. These include your Durable General Power of Attorney, Durable Power of Attorney for Healthcare and Directive to Physicians. Remember to send copies of all these forms to your healthcare agencies so they will have them on file if needed. Your attorney and designated conservator/trustee also get copies. Some people with strong religious convictions give a copy to their clergy as well, so their clergy may reassure family members that this truly was what the grantor wanted.

Once you have put your trust notebook together, find a safe place for it in your house. Make sure all family members know where it is. If for any reason the notebook or some of the documents get destroyed, replace them immediately.

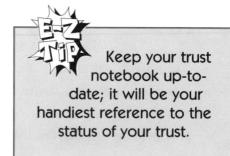

Keep your trust notebook up-to-date; it will be your handiest reference to the status of your trust.

Amending your trust

Sometimes events occur that make it necessary to amend a trust agreement. You may outlive your successor trustee, for example, or that person could become mentally or physically incapacitated and unable to preside over the trust. You may also outlive or have a falling out with one or more of your beneficiaries.

To change a trustee or beneficiary, attach an amendment to your revocable living trust. (Specific directions for wording such an amendment may be found in the back of this guide.) Staple all such amendments to the front of the trust so they may easily be seen. You must also file the amendment at the county recorder's office where you filed your original Certificate of Trustees' Powers.

note As grantor, you retain the right during your lifetime to appoint and fire trustees as you see fit; a trustee may not object to your removing him or her from the trust agreement. (Exception: if you have made your spouse co-trustee, it will be difficult to remove him or her from the trust agreement without terminating the trust itself.) A trustee may also choose to resign, in which case you will have to appoint someone to take his or her place. An amendment is easy to file at any time, as long as you are of sound mind.

Occasionally it becomes necessary to amend the trust to include new conditions. Always have your attorney draw up such an amendment to ensure it is properly worded. The amendment will then be stapled to the revocable living trust, dated, and numbered to show which part of the agreement it pertains to.

note If you are changing language contained in the Certificate of Trustees' Powers, you must file the amendment with the county recorder's office where the original certificate is filed; otherwise, simply staple the Amendment to Trust form to the revocable living trust.

If you want to delete something from your trust agreement, use the Amendment to Trust form provided in this guide. Fill in the number of the paragraph you want to delete from the revocable living trust. Check with your attorney to make sure it is done correctly.

You may also use the Amendment to Trust form to change the wording of a paragraph. State the number of the paragraph you want to delete; then state that you are substituting the following new paragraph in its place, and write out the new paragraph.

Most changes require the approval of all co-trustees. This is one reason for choosing co-trustees you know well.

Terminating a trust

Although a revocable living trust provides the best of all worlds, situations occur when you may need to terminate your agreement. Divorce is one of the most common situations. Consult your attorney immediately if you have a trust and your marriage is ending, particularly if your spouse is co-trustee. This is especially important in community property states, where a judge will assume all property included in trust to be community property unless you and your spouse immediately form separate trusts.

The only way to end a trust officially is to file a Revocation of Trust and record it in your county recorder's office. You must officially file the Revocation of Trust as proof that your trust no longer legally exists.

note
Filing a new will does not end your trust; neither does transferring the assets back into your own name.

Once you die, the trust becomes irrevocable and changing trustees or beneficiaries is more complex. If your successor trustee dies, becomes incompetent or chooses to resign his or her duties, an Affidavit of Succession stating a new trustee has assumed those duties must be filed at the county recorder's office. Proof of death or notes from physicians confirming incompetence must be attached to the affidavit.

note
If it becomes necessary to terminate the trust after your death, a surviving grantor or successor trustee may transfer all property from the trust using the Assignment of Property form and file a Revocation of Trust. However, this only empties the trust—it does not really end it according to established legal terms. Every party involved in the trust must approve its revocation for the trust to end when a grantor is no longer living. A probate judge must then review the reasons for the termination. If the judge believes that ending the trust will not conflict with the grantor's intentions, the request is approved and an order terminating the trust is issued. The order is then attached to the revocable living trust.

In reality there are few situations where such formal termination is needed. Usually a trust automatically ends when all of its assets have been distributed to the beneficiaries by the successor trustees. Always consult an attorney before legally ending a trust; there may be options available allowing you to hold it together.

note

A living trust is a good safety net for your property. With a little work on your part, your trust can protect all that you have worked for and guarantee that it will go to those you love.

Setting a timeline for your trust

7

Chapter 7

Setting a timeline for your trust

What you'll find in this chapter:

⟹ Scheduling the establishment of your trust

⟹ What to do if you file for divorce

⟹ Who to notify and when

⟹ Duties of successor trustees

⟹ Where to keep your trust

You may feel a bit overwhelmed by the work involved in forming and maintaining a living trust. In fact, most of the work takes place over a long period of time, allowing you to think through what you are doing and avoid mistakes. While you want to set up your trust as quickly as possible, you do not want—or need—to rush this process.

A checklist and review

The following checklist will help you remember all the steps you need to take. If it takes ten weeks to form your trust instead of the seven weeks listed below, don't worry; the important thing is that you are setting up a trust, and taking the time to do it right.

Week 1

Discuss with your family their present and future financial needs and how a trust will provide for them. Decide who will get what, who will act as your co- and successor trustees, which charities you are leaving your money to, who will make your healthcare decisions, and who will act as guardians for your minor children.

Consider who you will choose as your trust attorney. Ask friends and relatives with trusts for references if necessary.

Locate important documents such as deeds, stock certificates, insurance policies, copyrights, and car registrations.

Week 2

Draw up your preliminary Schedule of Assets. Include all your money, real estate, intangibles, insurance payable to the estate, and personal property; single persons should include their cars. Subtract mortgages, debts, liens, and other liabilities to estimate your estate's net worth. List each asset's physical description, location, type of ownership, what it does, and what it's worth. Get items appraised if their present value is questionable.

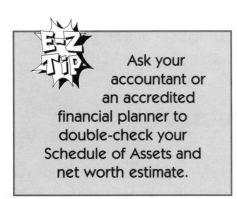

Ask your accountant or an accredited financial planner to double-check your Schedule of Assets and net worth estimate.

Make copies of the trust documents provided in this guide. Fill them in the way you think you want the trust agreement to read; place with other legal documents to take to your attorney's office.

Week 3

Meet with bank officials to set up a separate trust account (if finances exceed probate limit). Get a safe deposit box. If an advisor is available to you, ask for advice on your Schedule of Assets and estimated net worth.

Meet with a trust attorney and ask about fees and other issues. If you feel comfortable working with the attorney, show him or her the documents you have filled out so far. Ask what other documents you must bring to the next meeting. Also inquire about the marital tax deduction for setting up an A-B or A-B-C Living Trust.

Week 4

Call your local Registry of Deeds for filing requirements and fees. (Your attorney may or may not handle this.) Contact your stock broker about transferring title to the trust for all stocks and bonds.

If you have an outstanding mortgage, notify your lender of your intentions to form the trust. Call your insurance agent and fill him or her in about the trust; ask if any special arrangements need to be made.

Week 5

Purchase a sturdy loose-leaf notebook to hold documents. Set up sections according to instructions in Chapter 6 (or whatever set-up works best for you and your family).

Meet with your attorney to sign and notarize all legal documents. Put originals in your safe deposit box; keep copies in the loose-leaf notebook.

Week 6

Send copies of your Certificate of Trustees' Powers to your county recorder if your attorney has not already done so. Send copies of all trust agreement documents to your family, beneficiaries, co-trustees, and successor trustees. Send copies of your Durable Power of Attorney for Healthcare and Directive to Physicians to all healthcare agencies you use. If applicable, consider giving a copy to your clergy, too.

Call each agency for the name of the proper contact person; check back to make sure the documents are received and have been put in your file.

Week 7

Go through your trust notebook with your family; explain what everything is and answer any questions.

Review the distribution of property with your successor trustees and make sure you all have the same understanding of how property will be distributed after your death. Discuss the tax forms to be filed and other legalities; ask your successor trustees to contact your attorney with any questions.

Once a year at tax time

Review additions to and deletions from the trust with your co- and successor trustees. Discuss any plans that may affect trust property and also bring up any changes in the family situation or new amendments to the agreement that will affect property distribution.

Every day

If you buy something for or sell something from the trust, file a Bill of Sale or Assignment of Property form in your trust notebook. Add all new property to your Schedule of Assets; delete sold property.

Special situations

- ***If you file for divorce***
  Speak to your attorney immediately about ending a trust that is jointly held with your spouse, especially if you live in a community property state.

- ***If you need to amend the trust***
  Call your attorney to get the correct wording. Staple the new amendment to the front of the Revocable Living Trust; also send a copy to your county recorder's office where the Certificate of Trustees' Powers is registered.

- ***If you must appoint a new trustee***
  File an amendment with your county recorder's office; staple the amendment to the front of the Revocable Living Trust.

- ***Appointing a new trustee when grantor is no longer living***
  File an Affidavit of Succession with the county recorder's office; staple it to the front of the Revocable Living Trust.

- ***Disinheriting a child as a beneficiary***
  Give a signed note to your attorney stating your reasons for disinheritance.

- *Changing conservators or healthcare decision makers*
  File a new Durable General Power of Attorney, Durable Power of Attorney for Healthcare and Directive to Physicians; file an Amendment to Trust to change the conservator; make certain all healthcare agencies and other parties get a copy.

- *Ending a trust while the grantor is still living*
  See your attorney; file a Revocation of Trust to make it official.

- *Ending a trust when grantor is no longer living*
  A judge must approve the reasons for the revocation.

Duties of the successor trustees

- Refer to the Letter of Instruction provided by grantor; call the trust attorney if necessary.

- Notify insurance firms, banks, stock brokers, mortgage lenders; check on IRA or veteran's benefits, if applicable; also check on Social Security benefits.

- Transfer title of bank accounts and other property to successor trustee (stop credit cards if in grantor's name alone).

- Review and pay all debts owed by grantor.

- Contact beneficiaries and distribute property.

- Get a separate tax ID number for A-B and A-B-C Trusts; file estate tax and other forms within one year of taking over as the successor trustee.

The forms in this guide

About These E-Z Legal Forms:
While the legal forms and documents in this product generally conform to the requirements of courts nationwide, certain courts may have additional requirements. Before completing and filing the forms in this product, check with the clerk of the court concerning these requirements.

ASSIGNMENT OF PROPERTY TO TRUST

Grantor(s): , does(do)
hereby sell, transfer and convey unto , as Trustee(s) of
, a revocable living trust dated

, (year).

The Property transferred consists of:

To have and to hold for the benefit of the trust, its beneficiaries, successors and assigns. Seller warrants to defend the sale of property against all and every person claiming an adverse interest to same.

Signed this day of , (year).

In presence of:

_____   _____

Witness   Grantor

_____   _____

Witness   Grantor

CERTIFICATE OF TRUSTEES' POWERS

The following is hereby certified:

Be it known that the undersigned, is/are Trustee(s) of   Trust, a trust executed by   (Grantor(s)) under the laws of the state of   and dated   .

Said Trustee(s) has(ve) the power to buy, sell, lease, invest or otherwise manage property owned by said trust.

Signed this   day of   ,   (year).

_____
Trustee

_____
Trustee

STATE OF

COUNTY OF   }

On   before me,   ,

personally appeared   ,

personally known to me (or proved to me on the basis of satisfactory evidence) to be the person(s) whose name(s) is/are subscribed to the within instrument and acknowledged to me that he/she/they executed the same in his/her/their authorized capacity(ies), and that by his/her/their signature(s) on the instrument the person(s), or the entity upon behalf of which the person(s) acted, executed the instrument. WITNESS my hand and official seal.

Signature _____   Affiant ___Known ___Produced ID

       Notary Public   ID Produced _____

                                                                         (Seal)

REVOCABLE ONE-PARTY LIVING TRUST

Known as

_____

Date:

Agreement made and executed this   day of   ,   (year)
by and between   , hereinafter referred to as the Grantor,
and   , hereinafter referred to as the Trustee.

If the above-named trustee should be unable to serve due to death, incapacity or unwillingness, Grantor   names a successor Trustee,

                          , of

with all the rights and duties as stated herein.

Grantor desires to create a revocable trust of the property described in Schedule A hereto
annexed, together with such monies, and other assets as the Trustee may hereafter at any time hold
or acquire hereunder (hereinafter referred to collectively as the "Trust Estate") for the purposes hereinafter set forth.

NOW, THEREFORE, in consideration of the premises and of the mutual covenants herein
contained, the Grantor agrees to execute such further instruments as shall be necessary to vest the
Trustee with full title to the property, and the Trustee agrees to hold the Trust Estate, IN TRUST,
NEVERTHELESS, for the following uses and purposes and subject to the terms and conditions hereinafter set forth:

The Trustee shall hold, manage, invest and reinvest the Trust Estate (if any requires such management and investment) and shall collect the income, if any, therefrom and shall dispose of the net
income and principal as follows:

I

(1)   During the lifetime of the Grantor, the Trustee shall pay to or apply for the benefit of the
Grantor all the net income from the Trust.

(2)   During the lifetime of the Grantor, the Trustee may pay to or apply for the benefit of the
Grantor such sums from the principal of this Trust as in its sole discretion shall be necessary or advisable from time to time for the medical care, comfortable maintenance and welfare of the Grantor, taking into consideration to the extent the Trustee deems advisable, any other income or resources of the
Grantor known to the Trustee.

(3)   The Grantor may at any time during his/her lifetime and from time to time, withdraw all or
any part of the principal of this Trust, free of trust, by delivering an instrument in writing duly signed
by him/her to the Trustee, describing the property or portion thereof desired to be withdrawn. Upon
receipt of such instrument, the Trustee shall thereupon convey and deliver to the Grantor, free of trust,
the property described in such instrument.

(4)   In the event the Grantor is adjudicated to be incompetent or in the event the Grantor is not
adjudicated incompetent, but by reason of illness or mental or physical disability is, in the opinion of
the Trustee, unable to properly handle his/her own affairs, then and in that event the Trustee may, during the Grantor's lifetime, pay to or apply for the benefit of the Grantor such sums from the net
income and from the principal of this Trust as are deemed necessary or advisable by the Trustee.

(5)   The interests of the Grantor shall be considered primary and superior to the interests of any beneficiary.

II

The Grantor reserves and shall have the exclusive right any time and from time to time during his/her lifetime by instrument in writing signed by the Grantor and delivered to the Trustee to modify or alter this Agreement, in whole or in part, without the consent of the Trustee or any beneficiary provided that the duties, powers and liabilities of the Trustee shall not be changed without his/her consent; and the Grantor reserves and shall have the right during his/her lifetime, by instrument in writing, signed by the Grantor and delivered to the Trustee, to cancel and annul this Agreement without the consent of the Trustee or any beneficiary hereof. Grantor expressly reserves the right to appoint successor trustees, replace present trustees and change the beneficiaries or the rights to property due any beneficiary.

III

In addition to any powers granted under applicable law or otherwise, and not in limitation of such powers, but subject to any rights and powers which may be reserved expressly by the Grantor in this Agreement, the Trustee is authorized to exercise the following powers to the Trustee's sole and absolute discretion.

a.   To hold and retain any or all property, real, personal, or mixed, received from the Grantor's estate, or from any other source, regardless of any law or rule of court relating to diversification, or non-productivity, for such time as the Trustee shall deem best, and to dispose of such property by sale, exchange, or otherwise, as and when deemed advisable; not withstanding this provision or any other contained herein.

b.   To sell, assign, exchange, transfer, partition and convey, or otherwise dispose of, any property, real, personal or mixed, which may be included in or may at any time become part of the Trust Estate, upon such terms and conditions as deemed advisable, at either public or private sale, including options and sales on credit and for the purpose of selling, assigning, exchanging, transferring, partitioning or conveying the same, to make, execute, acknowledge, and deliver any and all instruments of conveyance, deeds of trust, and assignments in such form and with such warranties and covenants as deemed expedient and proper; and in the event of any sale, conveyance or other disposition of any of the Trust Estate, the purchaser shall not be obligated in any way to see the application of the purchase money or other consideration passing in connection therewith.

c.   To lease or rent and manage any or all of the real estate, which may be included in or at any time become a part of the Trust Estate, upon such terms and conditions deemed advisable, irrespective of whether the term of the lease shall exceed the period permitted by law or the probable period of any trust created hereby, and to review and modify such leases; and for the purpose of leasing said real estate, to make, execute, acknowledge and deliver any and all instruments in such form and with such covenants and warranties as deemed expedient and proper; and to make any repairs, replacements, and improvements, structural and otherwise, of any property, and to charge the expense thereof in an equitable manner to principal or income, as deemed proper.

d.   To borrow money for any purpose in connection with said Trust created hereby, and to execute promissory notes or other obligations for amounts so borrowed, and to secure the payment of any such amounts by mortgage or pledge or any real or personal property, and to renew or extend the time of payment of any obligation, secured or unsecured, payable to or by any trust created hereby, for such periods of time as deemed advisable.

e.   To invest and reinvest or leave temporarily uninvested any or all of the funds of the Trust Estate as said Trustee in the Trustee's sole discretion may deem best, including investments in stocks, common and preferred, and common trust fund, without being restricted to those investments expressly approved by statute for investment by fiduciaries, and to change investments from realty to personalty, and vice versa.

f.   To compromise, adjust, arbitrate, sue or defend, abandon, or otherwise deal with and settle claims, in favor of or against the Trust Estate as the Trustee shall deem best and the Trustee's decision shall be conclusive.

g.   To determine in a fair and reasonable manner whether any part of the Trust Estate, or any addition or increment thereto be income or principal, or whether any cost, charge, expense, tax, or assessment shall be charged against income or principal, or partially against income and partially against principal.

h.   To engage and compensate, out of principal or income or both, as equitably determined, agents, accountants, brokers, attorneys-in-fact, attorneys-at-law, tax specialists, realtors, custodians, investment counsel, and other assistants and advisors, and to do so without liability for any neglect, omission, misconduct, or default of any such agent or professional representative, provided he or she was selected and retained with reasonable care.

i.   To vote any stock, bonds, or other securities held by the Trust at any meetings of stockholders, bondholders, or other security holders and to delegate the power so to vote to attorneys- in-fact or proxies under power of attorney, restricted or unrestricted, and to join in or become party to any organization, readjustment, voting trust, consideration or exchange, and to deposit securities with any persons, and to pay any fees incurred in connection therewith, and to charge the same to principal or income, as deemed proper, and to exercise all of the rights with regard to such securities.

j.   To purchase securities, real estate, or other property from the executor or other personal representative of the Grantor's estate and the Trustees of any agreement or declaration executed by the Grantor during his/her lifetime under his/her last will in case his/her executors or Trustees are in need of cash, liquid assets, or income-producing assets with which to pay taxes, claims, or other estate or trust indebtedness, or in case such executors or Trustees are in need of such property to properly exercise and discharge their discretion with respect to distributions to beneficiaries as provided for under such bills, declarations, or agreements. Such purchase may be in cash or may be in exchange for other property of this Trust, and the Trustees shall not be liable in any way for any loss resulting to the Trust Estate by reason of the exercise of said authority.

k.   To undertake such further acts as are incidental to any of the foregoing or are reasonably required to carry out the tenor, purpose and intent of the Trust.

l.   To make loans or advancements to the executor or other personal representative of the Grantor's estate and the Trustees of any agreement or declaration executed by the Grantor during his/her lifetime or under his/her last will in case such executors or Trustees are in need of cash for any reason. Such loans or advancements may be secured or unsecured, and the Trustees shall not be liable in any way for any loss resulting to the Trust Estate by reason of the exercise of this authority.

IV

Upon death of the Grantor, the remaining Trust assets shall be distributed to the beneficiaries in the proportionate or allocable amounts as are specified in the Schedule of Beneficiaries as may then be in force.

If any beneficiary and the Grantor should die under such circumstances as would render it doubtful whether the beneficiary or the Grantor died first, then it shall be conclusively presumed for the purposes of this Trust that said beneficiary predeceased the Grantor.

V

If it shall be determined that any provision of the Trust created herein violates any rule against perpetuities or remoteness of vesting now or hereafter in effect in a governing jurisdiction, that portion of the Trust herein created shall be administered as herein provided until the termination of the maximum period allowed by law at which time and forthwith such part of the Trust shall be distributed in fee simple to the beneficiaries then entitled to receive income therefrom, and for the purpose, it shall be presumed that any beneficiary entitled to receive support or education from the income or principal of any particular fund is entitled to receive the income therefrom.

VI

Except as otherwise provided herein, all payments of principal and income payable, or to become payable, to the beneficiary of any trust created hereunder shall not be subject to anticipation, assignment, pledge, sale or transfer in any manner, nor shall any said beneficiary have the power to anticipate or encumber such interest, nor shall such interest, while in possession of the Trustee, be liable for, or subject to, the debts, contracts, obligations, liabilities or torts of any beneficiary.

VII

This Trust Agreement shall be construed, regulated and governed by and in accordance with the laws of the State of   .

I certify that I have read the foregoing Trust Agreement and that it correctly states the terms and conditions under which the Trust Estate is to be held, managed and disposed of by the Trustee.

Dated: _____

Grantor

_____

Trustee

WITNESSES:

The grantor has signed this trust at the end and has declared or signified in our presence that it is his/her revocable living trust, and in the presence of the grantor and each other we have hereunto subscribed our names this _____ day of _____ , _____ .

_____   _____
Witness Signature   Address

_____   _____
Witness Signature   Address

_____   _____
Witness Signature   Address

We,_____,_____,
_____ , and_____ , the grantors and the witnesses, respectively, whose names are signed to the attached and foregoing instrument were sworn and declared to the undersigned that the grantor signed the instrument as his/her revocable living trust and that each of the witnesses, in the presence of the grantor and each other, signed the trust as witnesses.

Grantor:_____   Witness:_____

                                                                       Witness:_____

                                                                       Witness:_____

STATE OF   }
COUNTY OF   }

On _____ before me, _____ , personally appeared _____ , grantor, _____ , witness, _____ , witness, _____ ,witness, personally known to me (or proved to me on the basis of satisfactory evidence) to be the person(s) whose name(s) is/are subscribed to the within instrument and acknowledged to me that he/she/they executed the same in his/her/their authorized capacity(ies), and that by his/her/their signature(s) on the instrument the person(s), or the entity upon behalf of which the person(s) acted, executed the instrument. WITNESS my hand and official seal.

Signature _____   Affiant ___Known ___Produced ID
            Notary Public   ID Produced _____

                                                                              (Seal)

REVOCABLE TWO-PARTY LIVING TRUST

Known as

_____

Date:

Agreement made and executed this   day of   ,   (year) by and between   , hereinafter referred to as the Grantors, and   , hereinafter referred to as the Trustees.

The first Grantor to die shall be called the "deceased Grantor." The living Grantor shall be called the "surviving Grantor." Upon the death of the deceased Grantor, the surviving Grantor shall serve as sole Trustee. In the event one of the Trustees is unable to perform the duties of a Trustee then the co- Trustee shall be the sole Trustee.

In the event the sole Trustee is unable to serve due to death, incapacity or unwillingness, Grantors name successor Trustee,   , of   with all rights and duties as stated herein.

Grantors desire to create a revocable trust of the property described in Schedule A hereto annexed, together with such monies, and other assets as the Trustees may hereafter at any time hold or acquire hereunder (hereinafter referred to collectively as the "Trust Estate") for the purposes hereinafter set forth.

NOW, THEREFORE, in consideration of the premises and of the mutual covenants herein contained, the Grantors agree to execute such further instruments as shall be necessary to vest the Trustees with full title to the property, and the Trustees agree to hold the Trust Estate, IN TRUST, NEVERTHELESS, for the following uses and purposes and subject to the terms and conditions hereinafter set forth:

The Trustees shall hold, manage, invest and reinvest the Trust Estate (if any requires such management and investment) and shall collect the income, if any, therefrom and shall dispose of the net income and principal as follows:

I

(1)   During the lifetime of the Grantors, the Trustees shall pay to or apply for the benefit of the Grantors all the net income from the Trust.

(2)   During the lifetime of the Grantors, the Trustees may pay to or apply for the benefit of the Grantors such sums from the principal of this Trust as in the Trustees' sole discretion shall be necessary or advisable from time to time for the medical care, comfortable maintenance and welfare of the Grantors, taking into consideration to the extent the Trustees deem advisable, any other income or resources of the Grantors known to the Trustees.

(3)   The Grantors may at any time during their lifetime and from time to time, withdraw all or any part of the principal of this Trust, free of trust, by delivering an instrument in writing duly signed by them to the Trustees, describing the property or portion thereof desired to be withdrawn. Upon receipt of such instrument, the Trustees shall thereupon convey and deliver to the Grantors, free of trust, the property described in such instrument.

(4)   In the event a Grantor is adjudicated to be incompetent or in the event a Grantor is not adjudicated incompetent, but by reason of illness or mental or physical disability is, in the opinion of the Trustees, unable to properly handle his/her own affairs, then and in that event the Trustees may during the Grantor's lifetime, in addition to the payments of income and principal for the benefit of the Grantor, pay to or apply for the benefit of the Grantor's spouse and any one or more of the Grantor's minor children, such sums from the net income and from the principal of this Trust in such shares and proportions as in the Trustees' sole discretion are determined to be necessary or advisable from time to time for the medical care, comfortable maintenance and welfare of the Grantor's said spouse and children taking into consideration to the extent the Trustees deem advisable, any other income or resources of the Grantor's said spouse and minor children known to the Trustee.

(5)   The interests of the Grantors shall be considered primary and superior to the interests of any beneficiary.

II

The Grantors reserve and shall have the exclusive right any time and from time to time during their lifetimes by instrument in writing signed by the Grantors and delivered to the Trustees to modify or alter this Agreement, in whole or in part, without the consent of the Trustees or any beneficiary provided that the duties, powers and liabilities of the Trustees shall not be changed without their consent; and the Grantors reserve and shall have the right during their lifetime, by instrument in writing, signed by the Grantors and delivered to the Trustees, to cancel and annul this Agreement without the consent of the Trustees or any beneficiary hereof. Grantors expressly reserve the right to appoint successor trustees, replace present trustees and change the beneficiaries or the rights to property due any beneficiary.

III

In addition to any powers granted under applicable law or otherwise, and not in limitation of such powers, but subject to any rights and powers which may be reserved expressly by the Grantors in this Agreement, the Trustees are authorized to exercise the following powers to the Trustees' sole and absolute discretion.

a.   To hold and retain any or all property, real, personal, or mixed, received from the Grantors' estate, or from any other source, regardless of any law or rule of court relating to diversification, or non-productivity, for such time as the Trustees shall deem best, and to dispose of such property by sale, exchange, or otherwise, as and when they shall deem advisable; not withstanding this provision or any other contained herein.

b.   To sell, assign, exchange, transfer, partition and convey, or otherwise dispose of, any property, real, personal or mixed, which may be included in or may at any time become part of the Trust Estate, upon such terms and conditions as deemed advisable, at either public or private sale, including options and sales on credit and for the purpose of selling, assigning, exchanging, transferring, partitioning or conveying the same, to make, execute, acknowledge, and deliver any and all instruments of conveyance, deeds of trust, and assignments in such form and with such warranties and covenants as they may deem expedient and proper; and in the event of any sale, conveyance or other disposition of any of the Trust Estate, the purchaser shall not be obligated in any way to see the application of the purchase money or other consideration passing in connection therewith.

c.   To lease or rent and manage any or all of the real estate, which may be included in or at any time become a part of the Trust Estate, upon such terms and conditions deemed advisable, irrespective of whether the term of the lease shall exceed the period permitted by law or the probable period of any trust created hereby, and to review and modify such leases; and for the purpose of leasing said real estate, to make, execute, acknowledge and deliver any and all instruments in such form and with such covenants and warranties as they may deem expedient and proper; and to make any repairs, replacements, and improvements, structural and otherwise, of any property, and to charge the expense thereof in an equitable manner to principal or income, as deemed proper.

   d. To borrow money for any purpose in connection with said Trust created hereby, and to execute promissory notes or other obligations for amounts so borrowed, and to secure the payment of any such amounts by mortgage or pledge or any real or personal property, and to renew or extend the time of payment of any obligation, secured or unsecured, payable to or by any trust created hereby, for such periods of time as deemed advisable.

   e. To invest and reinvest or leave temporarily uninvested any or all of the funds of the Trust Estate as said Trustees in the Trustees' sole discretion may deem best, including investments in stocks, common and preferred, and common trust fund, without being restricted to those investments expressly approved by statute for investment by fiduciaries, and to change investments from realty to personalty, and vice versa.

   f. To compromise, adjust, arbitrate, sue or defend, abandon, or otherwise deal with and settle claims, in favor of or against the Trust Estate as the Trustees shall deem best and the Trustees' decision shall be conclusive.

   g. To determine in a fair and reasonable manner whether any part of the Trust Estate, or any addition or increment thereto be income or principal, or whether any cost, charge, expense, tax, or assessment shall be charged against income or principal, or partially against income and partially against principal.

   h. To engage and compensate, out of principal or income or both, as equitably determined, agents, accountants, brokers, attorneys-in-fact, attorneys-at-law, tax specialists, realtors, custodians, investment counsel, and other assistants and advisors, and to do so without liability for any neglect, omission, misconduct, or default of any such agent or professional representative, provided he or she was selected and retained with reasonable care.

   i. To vote any stock, bonds, or other securities held by the Trust at any meetings of stockholders, bondholders, or other security holders and to delegate the power so to vote to attorneys- in-fact or proxies under power of attorney, restricted or unrestricted, and to join in or become party to any organization, readjustment, voting trust, consideration or exchange, and to deposit securities with any persons, and to pay any fees incurred in connection therewith, and to charge the same to principal or income, as deemed proper, and to exercise all of the rights with regard to such securities.

   j. To purchase securities, real estate, or other property from the executor or other personal representative of the Grantors' estate, the executor or other personal representative of the Grantors' spouse's estate, and the Trustees of any agreement or declaration executed by the Grantors during their lifetimes under their last wills in case their executors or Trustees are in need of cash, liquid assets, or income-producing assets with which to pay taxes, claims, or other estate or trust indebtedness, or in case such executors or Trustees are in need of such property to properly exercise and discharge their discretion with respect to distributions to beneficiaries as provided for under such bills, declarations, or agreements. Such purchase may be in cash or may be in exchange for other property of this Trust, and the Trustees shall not be liable in any way for any loss resulting to the Trust Estate by reason of the exercise of said authority.

   k. To undertake such further acts as are incidental to any of the foregoing or are reasonably required to carry out the tenor, purpose and intent of the Trust.

   l. To make loans or advancements to the executor or other personal representative of the Grantors' estate, the executor or other personal representative of the Grantors' spouse's estate, and the

Trustees of any agreement or declaration executed by the Grantors during their lifetimes or under their last wills in case such executors or Trustees are in need of cash for any reason. Such loans or advancements may be secured or unsecured, and the Trustees shall not be liable in any way for any loss resulting to the Trust Estate by reason of the exercise of this authority.

IV

Upon death of the Grantors, or the last surviving Grantor if more than one, the remaining Trust assets shall be distributed to the beneficiaries in the proportionate or allocable amounts as are specified in the schedule of beneficiaries as may then be in force.

If any beneficiary and the Grantors should die under such circumstances as would render it doubtful whether the beneficiary or the Grantors died first, then it shall be conclusively presumed for the purposes of this Trust that said beneficiary predeceased the Grantors.

V

If it shall be determined that any provision of the Trust created herein violates any rule against perpetuities or remoteness of vesting now or hereafter in effect in a governing jurisdiction, that portion of the Trust herein created shall be administered as herein provided until the termination of the maximum period allowed by law at which time and forthwith such part of the Trust shall be distributed in fee simple to the beneficiaries then entitled to receive income therefrom, and for the purpose, it shall be presumed that any beneficiary entitled to receive support or education from the income or principal of any particular fund is entitled to receive the income therefrom.

VI

Except as otherwise provided herein, all payments of principal and income payable, or to become payable, to the beneficiary of any trust created hereunder shall not be subject to anticipation, assignment, pledge, sale or transfer in any manner, nor shall any said beneficiary have the power to anticipate or encumber such interest, nor shall such interest, while in possession of the Trustees, be liable for, or subject to, the debts, contracts, obligations, liabilities or torts of any beneficiary.

VII

This Trust Agreement shall be construed, regulated and governed by and in accordance with the laws of the State of   .

We certify that we have read the foregoing Trust Agreement and that it correctly states the terms and conditions under which the Trust Estate is to be held, managed and disposed of by the Trustees.

Dated:

_____   _____
Grantor   Trustee

_____   _____
Grantor   Trustee

WITNESSED:

The grantors have signed this trust at the end and have declared or signified in our presence that it is their revocable living trust, and in the presence of the grantors and each other we have hereunto subscribed our names this _____ day of _____ , _____ (year).

_____   _____
Witness Signature   Address

_____   _____
Witness Signature   Address

_____   _____
Witness Signature   Address

We, _____,_____,_____, _____, and _____, the grantors and the witnesses, respectively, whose names are signed to the attached and foregoing instrument, were sworn and declared to the undersigned that the grantors signed the instrument as their revocable living trust and that each of the witnesses, in the presence of the grantors and each other, signed the trust as witnesses:

Grantor:_____   Witness:_____

Grantor:_____   Witness:_____

                                                                   Witness:_____

STATE OF _____
COUNTY OF _____   }

On _____ before me, _____ , personally appeared _____ , grantors; _____ ,witness; _____ ,witness, _____ witness, personally known to me (or proved to me on the basis of satisfactory evidence) to be the person(s) whose name(s) is/are subscribed to the within instrument and acknowledged to me that he/she/they executed the same in his/her/their authorized capacity(ies), and that by his/her/their signature(s) on the instrument the person(s), or the entity upon behalf of which the person(s) acted, executed the instrument. WITNESS my hand and official seal.

Signature _____   Affiant ___Known ___Produced ID
           Notary Public   ID Produced _____

                                                                              (Seal)

SCHEDULE OF ASSETS

Name of Trust: Date of Trust:

No.	Date of transfer in	Asset transfered to trust	Form of ownership	Tax based on date of transfer	Fair Market Value on date of transfer

No.	Date of transfer in	Asset transfered to trust	Form of ownership	Tax based on date of transfer	Fair Market Value on date of transfer

The undersigned Grantor(s) has(ve) reviewed the Schedule of Assets and approve the form of ownership of property as set forth above this date: _____

_____   _____
Signature of Grantor   Signature of Grantor

SCHEDULE OF BENEFICIARIES
AND DISTRIBUTIVE SHARES

The following are the named beneficiaries of the
Trust, as of this   day of   ,   (year).

                                                                Property Distributed and
Name of Beneficiary   Quantity and/or Percent

AFFIDAVIT OF SUCCESSION

Be it known that the undersigned Successor Trustee, under a Revocable Living Trust execut-ed by _____ (Grantor(s)) on _____ , hereby states that he/she has assumed the duties of Successor Trustee as specified in said Trust and that said Grantor(s) is/are now incapacitated or deceased.

WHEREFORE, Successor Trustee has assumed title to the real property and/or other assets covered by said Trust and will hereafter administer the same in accordance with the instructions set forth in said Trust.

Signed this _____ day of _____ , _____ (year).

_____   _____
Witness   Successor Trustee under Trust

                                                                            executed by _____

_____   _____
Witness   Name of Grantor

                                                                            on _____

STATE OF
COUNTY OF   }

On _____ before me, _____ ,
personally appeared _____ ,
personally known to me (or proved to me on the basis of satisfactory evidence) to be the person(s) whose name(s) is/are subscribed to the within instrument and acknowledged to me that he/she/they executed the same in his/her/their authorized capacity(ies), and that by his/her/their signature(s) on the instrument the person(s), or the entity upon behalf of which the person(s) acted, executed the instrument. WITNESS my hand and official seal.

Signature _____   Affiant ___Known ___Produced ID

          Notary Public   ID Produced _____

                                                                                                              (Seal)

AMENDMENT TO TRUST NO._____

NAME OF TRUST:

Effective Date of Trust: Amendment Date:

Grantor(s):   Trustee(s):

(Hereinafter referred to   (Hereinafter referred to
as Grantor(s))   as Trustee(s))

The above-described trust, by and between the above-named Grantor(s) and Trustee(s), is amended by substituting, adding or deleting the following provisions:

Page _____ of _____.

All provisions of the above Trust are hereby incorporated by reference herein with the exception of the provisions expressly modified by this Amendment.

IN WITNESS WHEREOF, the parties hereto have duly executed this Amendment to the above Trust on date first above written.

_____   _____

_____   _____

Signature of Grantor(s)   Signature of Trustee(s)

This Trust Amendment was signed in the presence of us who, at the request and in the presence of Grantor(s) and in the presence of each other, have signed as witnesses thereto.

Witnesses:

_____

_____

_____

Signature of Witnesses

STATE OF

COUNTY OF   }

On   before me,   ,

personally appeared   ,

personally known to me (or proved to me on the basis of satisfactory evidence) to be the person(s) whose name(s) is/are subscribed to the within instrument and acknowledged to me that he/she/they executed the same in his/her/their authorized capacity(ies), and that by his/her/their signature(s) on the instrument the person(s), or the entity upon behalf of which the person(s) acted, executed the instrument. WITNESS my hand and official seal.

Signature _____   Affiant ___Known ___Produced ID

    Notary Public   ID Produced _____

                                                                                (Seal)

Page _____ of _____.

BILL OF SALE

BE IT KNOWN, for good consideration and in payment of the sum of $,
the receipt and sufficiency of which is acknowledged, the undersigned
                    of   (Seller) hereby
sells and transfers to   of
                    (Buyer) and the Buyer's successors and assigns forever, the following
described chattels and personal property:

The Seller warrants to Buyer it has good and marketable title to said property, full authority
to sell and transfer said property, and that said property is sold free of all liens, encumbrances, liabilities, and adverse claims of every nature and description whatsoever.

Seller further warrants to Buyer that it will fully defend, protect, indemnify and hold harm-
less the Buyer and its lawful successors and assigns from any adverse claim made thereto by all persons whomever.

Said property is otherwise sold in "as is" condition and where presently located.

Signed this   day of a   ,   (year).

Signed in the presence of:

_____   _____
Witness   Seller

Address _____

_____

_____

REVOCATION OF TRUST

The undersigned, _____ , as Grantor(s) of a certain revocable living trust entitled _____ Trust, dated _____ , (year), does/do hereby revoke said trust effective this date.

(1)   Notice: A copy of this revocation has been mailed to the below-named trustee(s):

And a further copy of this revocation has been mailed to the below-named beneficiary(ies):

(2)   Recording: A signed original of this notice of revocation shall or has been duly recorded with the county recorder's office in the following counties:

This revocation made under oath and the stated facts herein affirmed as true and correct this ____ day of _____ , _____ (year).

_____   _____
Grantor   Grantor

STATE OF   }
COUNTY OF

On _____ before me, _____ ,
personally appeared _____ ,
personally known to me (or proved to me on the basis of satisfactory evidence) to be the person(s) whose name(s) is/are subscribed to the within instrument and acknowledged to me that he/she/they executed the same in his/her/their authorized capacity(ies), and that by his/her/their signature(s) on the instrument the person(s), or the entity upon behalf of which the person(s) acted, executed the instrument. WITNESS my hand and official seal.

Signature _____   Affiant ___Known ___Produced ID
         Notary Public   ID Produced _____
                                                                                    (Seal)

Glossary of useful terms

A-As

A Trust

A single trust normally used by individuals and couples who have less than the Unified Tax Credit Exemption.

A-B Trust

A joint trust normally used by couples with between the single and the couple Unified Tax Credit Exemption.

A-B-C Trust

A second type of joint trust normally used by married couples whose estates exceed the maximum Unified Tax Credit Exemption, or who have children from previous marriages.

Affidavit of Succession

Filed when the grantor is no longer living and it is necessary to replace the successor trustee with a new trustee; must be filed with the county recorder.

Appreciation

The growth in value of property over time.

Asset

Property of value placed in trust.

As-C

Assignment of Property

The forms used to transfer title of property to a trust.

Beneficiary

A person who inherits property from an estate.

Certified Copy

A copy of a document with an official seal.

Certificate of Trustees' Powers

A document stating the powers of a grantor's appointed trustee(s) to buy, sell, lease, invest and otherwise manage trust property.

Commingled Funds

(1) When a grantor's personal funds get mixed in by mistake with trust funds; to be avoided at all costs. (2) When a husband and wife put their money in one account.

Community Property

A valid legal concept in nine states; all property earned by either the husband or wife during a marriage is automatically joint property.

Conservator

The person appointed to look after an adult who is unable to look after him or herself.

Contingent Beneficiary

Person named to receive property from an estate if the first-choice beneficiary is no longer living when property is distributed.

C-D

Co-Trustee

A second person entrusted with property for the benefit of others.

Creditor

A party to whom money is owed.

Curtesy State

One of several states in which a wife is required to leave at least one third of her property to her husband.

Directive to Physicians

A document that states how life support decisions should be handled if one is incapacitated.

Disinterested Trustee

An attorney, accountant or other professional who manages an estate; someone objective about financial and legal matters regarding a trust; often appointed along with a family member as successor trustees.

Dower State

One of several states that require a husband to leave at least a third of his property to his wife.

Durable General Power of Attorney

Gives another person the right to act on the grantor's behalf if the grantor becomes unable to make his or her own decisions.

Durable Healthcare Power of Attorney

Gives another person the right to make healthcare decisions for the grantor if the grantor becomes unable to speak for him or herself.

E-L

Estate Tax

Taxes charged to an estate over the Unified Tax Credit Exemption when its grantor is no longer living; may often be avoided by setting up a trust.

Executor/Executrix

The person appointed to manage an estate when a will is involved. Usually referred to as the personal representative.

Fixed Rate

One set fee for services rendered, rather than charging by the hour.

Grantor

The person who puts his or her property in trust; also known as the trustor.

Guardian

The person(s) appointed to look after minor children upon the death of the parent(s).

Insurance Trust

A specialized trust holding insurance policies or their proceeds.

Intangibles

Items of value that can't be physically touched—e.g., copyrights, patents and credit.

Joint Property

Property owned by two or more people.

Letter of Instruction

A letter from the grantor or grantor's attorney to the successor trustee(s) with instructions on what to do upon the grantor's death.

L-R

Living Trust

A legal arrangement whereby a person owning property (grantor) transfers title to a second person (trustee) for the benefit of a third person (beneficiary).

Net Worth

A person's total assets minus debts.

Notary Public

A person authorized to witness the signing of documents, verify that the signatures are genuine, and state that a document was actually signed on the reported date.

Planned Giving Officer

The person at a charitable institution who helps people make bequests to the organization. Smaller nonprofits may use a Development Officer to handle this.

Pour-Over Will

A document stating that all assets accidentally left out of trust when the grantor is no longer living should go into the trust. Anything in a pour-over will must go through probate.

Probate

The complicated process of administering a will; this may be avoided by forming a living trust. Probate is necessary for estates without trusts when there is more than $30,000 in property or $10,000 in real estate.

Retainer Fee

The fee paid to an attorney to guarantee that he or she will represent you.

R-T

Revocable Living Trust

The main document of a trust agreement; states an individual's intent to form a trust and names the parties involved.

Schedule of Assets

A list of all property to be kept in trust; includes each item's location, type of ownership, function, and worth.

Separate Property

Property purchased or inherited previous to a marriage in a community property state. If it is commingled with community property, it becomes community property.

Successor Trustees

The persons who take over management of a trust when the grantor is no longer living, and/or when the original trustee is no longer able to serve.

Termination of Trust Affidavit

Document a grantor files with the county recorder in order to end a trust. An attorney should be consulted.

Testamentary Trust

A trust that goes into effect after the grantor dies. Unlike a living trust, a testamentary trust does not protect an estate from probate.

Totten Trust

A bank account trust which bypasses probate and goes directly to the beneficiary upon the grantor's death.

T-U

Trustee

The person who takes title to property and manages a trust; this person may also be the grantor. If two people serve as co-trustees of a trust, both parties must approve all decisions.

Trust Notebook

The book in which an organized grantor keeps all forms and documents related to trust property.

Uniform Probate Code

A law that requires persons who live in certain states to record their trusts.

Unlimited Marital Deduction

Exempts an estate from having to pay estate taxes when the first spouse dies, if everything is left to the surviving spouse. The estate must pay a tax when the second spouse dies unless an A-B or A-B-C Living Trust is in place and the total estate is less than the Unified Tax Credit Exemption. The second spouse may help to ensure that the trust meets this limit by giving away money during his or her lifetime.

Resources

••• Online Resources •••

◆ **ABA Law Practice Management Section—Estate Planning and Probate Interest Group**

   URL: http://www.abanet.org/lpm/lpdiv/estate.html

◆ **American Academy of Estate Planning Attorneys, Inc.**

   URL: http://www.aaepa.com

◆ **American Association of Retired Persons Webplace**

   URL: http://www.aarp.org/getans/consumer/wills.html

◆ **California Estate Planning, Probate & Trust Law**

   URL: http://www.ca-probate.com

◆ **Choice in Dying**

URL: http://www.choices.org

◆ **Crash Course in Wills and Trusts**

URL: http://www.mtpalermo.com

◆ **Discovering and Obtaining Death Benefits**

URL: http://www.bluefin.net/~jtcmac

◆ **Estate Planning Links Web Site, The**

URL: http://hometown.aol.com/dmk58/eplinks.html

◆ **FindLaw**

URL: http://www.findlaw.com/01topics/31probate

◆ **Growth House, Inc.**

URL: http://www.growthhouse.org

◆ **Internet Law Library**

URL: http://hometown.aol.com/dmk58/eplinks.html

◆ **Law & Estate Planning Sites on the Internet**

URL: http://www.ca-probate.com/links.htm

◆ **Law Journal Extra!**

URL: http://www.ljx.com/practice/trusts/index.html

◆ **Legal Information Institute**

   URL: http://www.law.cornell.edu/topics/state_statutes.html
   #probate

◆ **'Lectric Law Library**

   URL: http://www.lectlaw.com

◆ **National Association of Financial and Estate Planning**

   URL: http://www.nafep.com

◆ **Ralf's 'Lectric Law Library Tour**

   URL: http://www.lectlaw.com/formb.htm

◆ **University of New England Law School**

   URL: http://www.anu.edu.au/law/pub/edinst/une
   /LS240TOPIC8.html

◆ **WebTrust.com**

   URL: http://www.webtrust.com/index.htm

◆ **Wills on the Web**

   URL: http://www.ca-probate.com/wills.htm

◆ **World Wide Web Virtual Library: Law: Property Law**

   URL: http://www.law.indiana.edu/law/v-lib/property.html

••• Related Sites •••

◆ **Institute of Certified Financial Planners**

URL: http://www.icfp.org

◆ **International Association for Financial Planning**

URL: http://www.iafp.org

◆ **National Association of Personal Financial Advisors**

URL: http://www.napfa.org

◆ **Pension and Welfare Benefits Administration**

URL: http://www.dol.gov/dol/pwba

••• Legal Search Engines •••

◆ **All Law**

http://www.alllaw.com

◆ **American Law Sources On Line**

http://www.lawsource.com/also/searchfm.htm

◆ **Catalaw**

http://www.catalaw.com

◆ **FindLaw**

  URL: http://www.findlaw.com

◆ **Hieros Gamos**

  http://www.hg.org/hg.html

◆ **InternetOracle**

  http://www.internetoracle.com/legal.htm

◆ **LawAid**

  http://www.lawaid.com/search.html

◆ **LawCrawler**

  http://www.lawcrawler.com

◆ **LawEngine, The**

  http://www.fastsearch.com/law

◆ **LawRunner**

  http://www.lawrunner.com

◆ **'Lectric Law Library**™

  http://www.lectlaw.com

◆ **Legal Search Engines**

http://www.dreamscape.com/frankvad/search.legal.html

◆ **LEXIS/NEXIS Communications Center**

http://www.lexis-nexis.com/lncc/general/search.html

◆ **Meta-Index for U.S. Legal Research**

http://gsulaw.gsu.edu/metaindex

◆ **Seamless Website, The**

http://seamless.com

◆ **USALaw**

http://www.usalaw.com/linksrch.cfm

◆ **WestLaw**

http://westdoc.com (Registered users only. Fee paid service.)

••• State Bar Associations •••

ALABAMA

Alabama State Bar
415 Dexter Avenue
Montgomery, AL 36104

mailing address:
PO Box 671
Montgomery, AL 36101
(205) 269-1515

http://www.alabar.org

ALASKA

Alaska Bar Association
510 L Street No. 602
Anchorage, AK 99501

mailing address
PO Box 100279
Anchorage, AK 99510

ARIZONA

State Bar of Arizona
111 West Monroe
Phoenix, AZ 85003-1742
(602) 252-4804

ARKANSAS

Arkansas Bar Association
400 West Markham
Little Rock, AR 72201
(501) 375-4605

CALIFORNIA

State Bar of California
555 Franklin Street
San Francisco, CA 94102
(415) 561-8200

http://www.calbar.org
Alameda County Bar
Association

http://www.acbanet.org

COLORADO

Colorado Bar Association
No. 950, 1900 Grant Street
Denver, CO 80203
(303) 860-1115

http://www.usa.net/cobar/
index.htm

CONNECTICUT

Connecticut Bar Association
101 Corporate Place
Rocky Hill, CT 06067-1894
(203) 721-0025

DELAWARE

Delaware State Bar Association
1225 King Street, 10th floor
Wilmington, DE 19801
(302) 658-5279
(302) 658-5278 (lawyer referral service)

DISTRICT OF COLUMBIA

District of Columbia Bar
1250 H Street, NW, 6th Floor
Washington, DC 20005
(202) 737-4700

Bar Association of the District of
Columbia
1819 H Street, NW, 12th floor
Washington, DC 20006-3690
(202) 223-6600

FLORIDA

The Florida Bar
The Florida Bar Center
650 Apalachee Parkway
Tallahassee, FL 32399-2300
(904) 561-5600

GEORGIA

State Bar of Georgia
800 The Hurt Building
50 Hurt Plaza
Atlanta, GA 30303
(404) 527-8700

*http://www.kuesterlaw.com/
comp.html*

HAWAII

Hawaii State Bar Association
1136 Union Mall
Penthouse 1
Honolulu, HI 96813
(808) 537-1868

http://www.hsba.org

IDAHO

Idaho State Bar
PO Box 895
Boise, ID 83701
(208) 334-4500

ILLINOIS

Illinois State Bar Association
424 South Second Street
Springfield, IL 62701
(217) 525-1760

INDIANA

Indiana State Bar Association
230 East Ohio Street
Indianapolis, IN 46204
(317) 639-5465

http://www.iquest.net/isba

IOWA

Iowa State Bar Association
521 East Locust
Des Moines, IA 50309
(515) 243-3179

http://www.iowabar.org

KANSAS

Kansas Bar Association
1200 Harrison Street
Topeka, KS 66601
(913) 234-5696

*http://www.ink.org/public/
cybar*

KENTUCKY

Kentucky Bar Association
514 West Main Street
Frankfort, KY 40601-1883
(502) 564-3795

http://www.kybar.org

LOUISIANA

Louisiana State Bar Association
601 St. Charles Avenue
New Orleans, LA 70130
(504) 566-1600

MAINE

Maine State Bar Association
124 State Street
PO Box 788
Augusta, ME 04330
(207) 622-7523

http://www.mainebar.org

MARYLAND

Maryland State Bar Association
520 West Fayette Street
Baltimore, MD 21201
(410) 685-7878

http://www.msba.org/msba

MASSACHUSETTS

Massachusetts Bar Association
20 West Street
Boston, MA 02111
(617) 542-3602
(617) 542-9103 (lawyer referral service)

MICHIGAN

State Bar of Michigan
306 Townsend Street
Lansing, MI 48933-2083
(517) 372-9030

http://www.umich.edu/~icle

MINNESOTA

Minnesota State Bar Association
514 Nicollet Mall
Minneapolis, MN 55402
(612) 333-1183

MISSISSIPPI

The Mississippi Bar
643 No. State Street
Jackson, Mississippi 39202
(601) 948-4471

MISSOURI

The Missouri Bar
P.O. Box 119, 326 Monroe
Jefferson City, Missouri 65102
(314) 635-4128

http://www.mobar.org

MONTANA

State Bar of Montana
46 North Main
PO Box 577
Helena, MT 59624
(406) 442-7660

NEBRASKA

Nebraska State Bar Association
635 South 14th Street, 2nd floor
Lincoln, NE 68508
(402) 475-7091

http://www.nol.org/legal/
nsba/index.html

NEVADA

State Bar of Nevada
201 Las Vegas Blvd.
Las Vegas, NV 89101
(702) 382-2200

http://www.dsi.org/statebar
/nevada.htm

NEW HAMPSHIRE

New Hampshire Bar Association
112 Pleasant Street
Concord, NH 03301
(603) 224-6942

NEW JERSEY

New Jersey State Bar Association
One Constitution Square
New Brunswuck, NJ 08901-1500
(908) 249-5000

NEW MEXICO

State Bar of New Mexico
121 Tijeras Street N.E.
Albuquerque, NM 87102

mailing address:
PO Box 25883
Albuquerque, NM 87125
(505) 843-6132

NEW YORK

New York State Bar Association
One Elk Street
Albany, NY 12207
(518) 463-3200

http://www.nysba.org

NORTH CAROLINA

North Carolina State Bar
208 Fayetteville Street Mall
Raleigh, NC 27601

mailing address:
PO Box 25908
Raleigh, NC 27611
(919) 828-4620

North Carolina Bar Association
1312 Annapolis Drive
Raleigh, NC 27608

mailing address:
PO Box 12806
Raleigh, NC 27605
(919) 828-0561

http://www.barlinc.org

NORTH DAKOTA

State Bar Association of North Dakota
515 1/2 East Broadway, suite 101
Bismarck, ND 58501

mailing address:
PO Box 2136
Bismarck, ND 58502
(701) 255-1404

OHIO

Ohio State Bar Association
1700 Lake Shore Drive
Columbus, OH 43204

mailing address:
PO Box 16562
Columbus, OH 43216-6562
(614) 487-2050

OKLAHOMA

Oklahoma Bar Association
1901 North Lincoln
Oklahoma City, OK 73105
(405) 524-2365

OREGON

Oregon State Bar
5200 S.W. Meadows Road
PO Box 1689
Lake Oswego, OR 97035-0889
(503) 620-0222

PENNSYLVANIA

Pennsylvannia Bar Association
100 South Street
PO Box 186
Harrisburg, PA 17108
(717) 238-6715

Pennsylvania Bar Institute
http://www.pbi.org

PUERTO RICO

Puerto Rico Bar Association
PO Box 1900
San Juan, Puerto Rico 00903
(809) 721-3358

RHODE ISLAND

Rhode Island Bar Association
115 Cedar Street
Providence, RI 02903
(401) 421-5740

SOUTH CAROLINA

South Carolina Bar
950 Taylor Street
PO Box 608
Columbia, SC 29202
(803) 799-6653

http://www.scbar.org

SOUTH DAKOTA

State Bar of South Dakota
222 East Capitol
Pierre, SD 57501
(605) 224-7554

TENNESSEE

Tennessee Bar Assn
3622 West End Avenue
Nashville, TN 37205
(615) 383-7421

http://www.tba.org

TEXAS

State Bar of Texas
1414 Colorado
PO Box 12487
Austin, TX 78711
(512) 463-1463

UTAH

Utah State Bar
645 South 200 East, Suite 310
Salt Lake City, UT 84111
(801) 531-9077

VERMONT

Vermont Bar Association
PO Box 100
Montpelier, VT 05601
(802) 223-2020

VIRGINIA

Virginia State Bar
707 East Main Street, suite 1500
Richmond, VA 23219-0501
(804) 775-0500

Virginia Bar Association
701 East Franklin St., Suite 1120
Richmond, VA 23219
(804) 644-0041

VIRGIN ISLANDS

Virgin Islands Bar Association
P.O. Box 4108
Christiansted, Virgin Islands
00822
(809) 778-7497

WASHINGTON

Washington State Bar
Association
500 Westin Street
2001 Sixth Avenue
Seattle, WA 98121-2599
(206) 727-8200

http://www.wsba.org

WEST VIRGINIA

West Virginia State Bar
2006 Kanawha Blvd. East
Charleston, WV 25311
(304) 558-2456

http://www.wvbar.org

West Virginia Bar Association
904 Security Building
100 Capitol Street
Charleston, WV 25301
(304) 342-1474

WISCONSIN

State Bar of Wisconsin
402 West Wilson Street
Madison, WI 53703
(608) 257-3838

http://www.wisbar.org/
home.htm

WYOMING

Wyoming State Bar
500 Randall Avenue
Cheyenne, WY 82001
PO Box 109
Cheyenne, WY 82003
(307) 632-9061

How to save on attorney fees

How to save on attorney fees

Millions of Americans know they need legal protection, whether it's to get agreements in writing, protect themselves from lawsuits, or document business transactions. But too often these basic but important legal matters are neglected because of something else millions of Americans know: legal services are expensive.

They don't have to be. In response to the demand for affordable legal protection and services, there are now specialized clinics that process simple documents. Paralegals help people prepare legal claims on a freelance basis. People find they can handle their own legal affairs with do-it-yourself legal guides and kits. Indeed, this book is a part of this growing trend.

When are these alternatives to a lawyer appropriate? If you hire an attorney, how can you make sure you're getting good advice for a reasonable fee? Most importantly, do you know how to lower your legal expenses?

When there is no alternative

Make no mistake: serious legal matters require a lawyer. The tips in this book can help you reduce your legal fees, but there is no alternative to good professional legal services in certain circumstances:

- when you are charged with a felony, you are a repeat offender, or jail is possible

- when a substantial amount of money or property is at stake in a lawsuit

- when you are a party in an adversarial divorce or custody case

- when you are an alien facing deportation

- when you are the plaintiff in a personal injury suit that involves large sums of money

- when you're involved in very important transactions

Are you sure you want to take it to court?

Consider the following questions before you pursue legal action:

What are your financial resources?

Money buys experienced attorneys, and experience wins over first-year lawyers and public defenders. Even with a strong case, you may save money by not going to court. Yes, people win millions in court. But for every big winner there are ten plaintiffs who either lose or win so little that litigation wasn't worth their effort.

Do you have the time and energy for a trial?

Courts are overbooked, and by the time your case is heard your initial zeal may have grown cold. If you can, make a reasonable settlement out of court. On personal matters, like a divorce or custody case, consider the emotional toll on all parties. Any legal case will affect you in some way. You will need time away from work. A newsworthy case may bring press coverage. Your loved ones, too, may face publicity. There is usually good reason to settle most cases quickly, quietly, and economically.

How can you settle disputes without litigation?

Consider *mediation*. In mediation, each party pays half the mediator's fee and, together, they attempt to work out a compromise informally. *Binding arbitration* is another alternative. For a small fee, a trained specialist serves as judge, hears both sides, and hands down a ruling that both parties have agreed to accept.

So you need an attorney

Having done your best to avoid litigation, if you still find yourself headed for court, you will need an attorney. To get the right attorney at a reasonable cost, be guided by these four questions:

What type of case is it?

You don't seek a foot doctor for a toothache. Find an attorney experienced in your type of legal problem. If you can get recommendations from clients who have recently won similar cases, do so.

Where will the trial be held?

You want a lawyer familiar with that court system and one who knows the court personnel and the local protocol—which can vary from one locality to another.

Should you hire a large or small firm?

Hiring a senior partner at a large and prestigious law firm sounds reassuring, but chances are the actual work will be handled by associates—at high rates. Small firms may give your case more attention but, with fewer resources, take longer to get the work done.

What can you afford?

Hire an attorney you can afford, of course, but know what a fee quote includes. High fees may reflect a firm's luxurious offices, high-paid staff and unmonitored expenses, while low estimates may mean "unexpected" costs later. Ask for a written estimate of all costs and anticipated expenses.

How to find a good lawyer

Whether you need an attorney quickly or you're simply open to future possibilities, here are seven nontraditional methods for finding your lawyer:

1) **Word of mouth**: Successful lawyers develop reputations. Your friends, business associates and other professionals are potential referral sources. But beware of hiring a friend. Keep the client-attorney relationship strictly business.

2) **Directories**: The Yellow Pages and the Martin-Hubbell Lawyer Directory (in your local library) can help you locate a lawyer with the right education, background and expertise for your case.

3) **Databases**: A paralegal should be able to run a quick computer search of local attorneys for you using the Westlaw or Lexis database.

4) **State bar associations**: Bar associations are listed in phone books. Along with lawyer referrals, your bar association can direct you to low-cost legal clinics or specialists in your area.

5) **Law schools**: Did you know that a legal clinic run by a law school gives law students hands-on experience? This may fit your legal needs. A third-year law student loaded with enthusiasm and a little experience might fill the bill quite inexpensively—or even for free.

6) **Advertisements**: Ads are a lawyer's business card. If a "TV attorney" seems to have a good track record with your kind of case, why not call? Just don't be swayed by the glamour of a high-profile attorney.

7) **Your own ad**: A small ad describing the qualifications and legal expertise you're seeking, placed in a local bar association journal, may get you just the lead you need.

How to hire and work with your attorney

No matter how you hear about an attorney, you must interview him or her in person. Call the office during business hours and ask to speak to the attorney directly. Then explain your case briefly and mention how you obtained the attorney's name. If the attorney sounds interested and knowledgeable, arrange for a visit.

The ten-point visit

1) Note the address. This is a good indication of the rates to expect.

2) Note the condition of the offices. File-laden desks and poorly maintained work space may indicate a poorly run firm.

3) Look for up-to-date computer equipment and an adequate complement of support personnel.

4) Note the appearance of the attorney. How will he or she impress a judge or jury?

5) Is the attorney attentive? Does the attorney take notes, ask questions, follow up on points you've mentioned?

6) Ask what schools he or she has graduated from, and feel free to check credentials with the state bar association.

7) Does the attorney have a good track record with your type of case?

8) Does he or she explain legal terms to you in plain English?

9) Are the firm's costs reasonable?

10) Will the attorney provide references?

Hiring the attorney

Having chosen your attorney, make sure all the terms are agreeable. Send letters to any other attorneys you have interviewed, thanking them for their time and interest in your case and explaining that you have retained another attorney's services.

Request a letter from your new attorney outlining your retainer agreement. The letter should list all fees you will be responsible for as well as the billing arrangement. Did you arrange to pay in installments? This should be noted in your retainer agreement.

Controlling legal costs

Legal fees and expenses can get out of control easily, but the client who is willing to put in the effort can keep legal costs manageable. Work out a budget with your attorney. Create a timeline for your case. Estimate the costs involved in each step.

Legal fees can be straightforward. Some lawyers charge a fixed rate for a specific project. Others charge contingency fees (they collect a percentage of your recovery, usually 35-50 percent if you win and nothing if you lose). But most attorneys prefer to bill by the hour. Expenses can run the gamut, with one hourly charge for taking depositions and another for making copies.

Have your attorney give you a list of charges for services rendered and an itemized monthly bill. The bill should explain the service performed, who performed the work, when the service was provided, how long it took, and how the service benefits your case.

Ample opportunity abounds in legal billing for dishonesty and greed. There is also plenty of opportunity for knowledgeable clients to cut their bills significantly if they know what to look for. Asking the right questions and setting limits on fees is smart and can save you a bundle. Don't be afraid to question legal bills. It's your case and your money!

When the bill arrives

- **Retainer fees**: You should already have a written retainer agreement. Ideally, the retainer fee applies toward case costs, and your agreement puts that in writing. Protect yourself by escrowing the retainer fee until the case has been handled to your satisfaction.

- **Office visit charges**: Track your case and all documents, correspondence, and bills. Diary all dates, deadlines and questions you want to ask your attorney during your next office visit. This keeps expensive office visits focused and productive, with more accomplished in less time. If your attorney charges less for phone consultations than office visits, reserve visits for those tasks that must be done in person.

- **Phone bills**: This is where itemized bills are essential. Who made the call, who was spoken to, what was discussed, when was the call made, and how long did it last? Question any charges that seem unnecessary or excessive (over 60 minutes).

- **Administrative costs**: Your case may involve hundreds, if not thousands, of documents: motions, affidavits, depositions, interrogatories, bills, memoranda, and letters. Are they all necessary? Understand your attorney's case strategy before paying for an endless stream of costly documents.

- **Associate and paralegal fees**: Note in your retainer agreement which staff people will have access to your file. Then you'll have an informed and efficient staff working on your case, and you'll recognize their names on your bill. Of course, your attorney should handle the important part of your case, but less costly paralegals or associates may handle routine matters more economically. Note: Some firms expect their associates to meet a quota of billable hours, although the time spent is not always warranted. Review your bill. Does the time spent make sense for the document in question? Are several staff involved in matters that should be handled by one person? Don't be afraid to ask questions. And withhold payment until you have satisfactory answers.

- **Court stenographer fees**: Depositions and court hearings require costly transcripts and stenographers. This means added expenses. Keep an eye on these costs.

- **Copying charges**: Your retainer fee should limit the number of copies made of your complete file. This is in your legal interest, because multiple files mean multiple chances others may access your confidential information. It is also in your financial interest, because copying costs can be astronomical.

- **Fax costs**: As with the phone and copier, the fax can easily run up costs. Set a limit.

- **Postage charges**: Be aware of how much it costs to send a legal document overnight, or a registered letter. Offer to pick up or deliver expensive items when it makes sense.

- **Filing fees**: Make it clear to your attorney that you want to minimize the number of court filings in your case. Watch your bill and question any filing that seems unnecessary.

- **Document production fee**: Turning over documents to your opponent is mandatory and expensive. If you're faced with reproducing boxes of documents, consider having the job done by a commercial firm rather than your attorney's office.

- **Research and investigations**: Pay only for photographs that can be used in court. Can you hire a photographer at a lower rate than what your attorney charges? Reserve that right in your retainer agreement. Database research can also be extensive and expensive; if your attorney uses Westlaw or Nexis, set limits on the research you will pay for.

- **Expert witnesses**: Question your attorney if you are expected to pay for more than a reasonable number of expert witnesses. Limit the number to what is essential to your case.

- **Technology costs**: Avoid videos, tape recordings, and graphics if you can use old-fashioned diagrams to illustrate your case.

- **Travel expenses**: Travel expenses for those connected to your case can be quite costly unless you set a maximum budget. Check all travel-related items on your bill, and make sure they are appropriate. Always question why the travel is necessary before you agree to pay for it.

- **Appeals costs**: Losing a case often means an appeal, but weigh the costs involved before you make that decision. If money is at stake, do a cost-benefit analysis to see if an appeal is financially justified.

- **Monetary damages**: Your attorney should be able to help you estimate the total damages you will have to pay if you lose a civil case. Always consider settling out of court rather than proceeding to trial when the trial costs will be high.

- **Surprise costs**: Surprise costs are so routine they're predictable. The judge may impose unexpected court orders on one or both sides, or the opposition will file an unexpected motion that increases your legal costs. Budget a few thousand dollars over what you estimate your case will cost. It usually is needed.

- **Padded expenses**: Assume your costs and expenses are legitimate. But some firms do inflate expenses—office supplies, database searches, copying, postage, phone bills—to bolster their bottom line. Request copies of bills your law firm receives from support services. If you are not the only client represented on a bill, determine those charges related to your case.

Keeping it legal without a lawyer

The best way to save legal costs is to avoid legal problems. There are hundreds of ways to decrease your chances of lawsuits and other nasty legal encounters. Most simply involve a little common sense. You can also use your own initiative to find and use the variety of self-help legal aid available to consumers.

11 situations in which you may not need a lawyer

1) **No-fault divorce**: Married couples with no children, minimal property, and no demands for alimony can take advantage of divorce mediation services. A lawyer should review your divorce agreement before you sign it, but you will have saved a fortune in attorney fees. A marital or family counselor may save a seemingly doomed marriage, or help both parties move beyond anger to a calm settlement. Either way, counseling can save you money.

2) **Wills**: Do-it-yourself wills and living trusts are ideal for people with estates of less than $600,000. Even if an attorney reviews your final documents, a will kit allows you to read the documents, ponder your bequests, fill out sample forms, and discuss your wishes with your family at your leisure, without a lawyer's meter running.

3) **Incorporating**: Incorporating a small business can be done by any business owner. Your state government office provides the forms and instructions necessary. A visit to your state office will probably be

necessary to perform a business name check. A fee of $100-$200 is usually charged for processing your Articles of Incorporation. The rest is paperwork: filling out forms correctly; holding regular, official meetings; and maintaining accurate records.

4) **Routine business transactions**: Copyrights, for example, can be applied for by asking the U.S. Copyright Office for the appropriate forms and brochures. The same is true of the U.S. Patent and Trademark Office. If your business does a great deal of document preparation and research, hire a certified paralegal rather than paying an attorney's rates. Consider mediation or binding arbitration rather than going to court for a business dispute. Hire a human resources/benefits administrator to head off disputes concerning discrimination or other employee charges.

5) **Repairing bad credit**: When money matters get out of hand, attorneys and bankruptcy should not be your first solution. Contact a credit counseling organization that will help you work out manageable payment plans so that everyone wins. It can also help you learn to manage your money better. A good company to start with is the Consumer Credit Counseling Service, 1-800-388-2227.

6) **Small Claims Court**: For legal grievances amounting to a few thousand dollars in damages, represent yourself in Small Claims Court. There is a small filing fee, forms to fill out, and several court visits necessary. If you can collect evidence, state your case in a clear and logical presentation, and come across as neat, respectful and sincere, you can succeed in Small Claims Court.

7) **Traffic Court**: Like Small Claims Court, Traffic Court may show more compassion to a defendant appearing without an attorney. If you are ticketed for a minor offense and want to take it to court, you will be asked to plead guilty or not guilty. If you plead guilty, you can ask for leniency in sentencing by presenting mitigating circumstances. Bring any witnesses who can support your story, and remember that presentation (some would call it acting ability) is as important as fact.

8) **Residential zoning petition**: If a homeowner wants to open a home business, build an addition, or make other changes that may affect his or her neighborhood, town approval is required. But you don't need a lawyer to fill out a zoning variance application, turn it in, and present your story at a public hearing. Getting local support before the hearing is the best way to assure a positive vote; contact as many neighbors as possible to reassure them that your plans won't adversely affect them or the neighborhood.

9) **Government benefit applications**: Applying for veterans' or unemployment benefits may be daunting, but the process doesn't require legal help. Apply for either immediately upon becoming eligible. Note: If your former employer contests your application for unemployment benefits and you have to defend yourself at a hearing, you may want to consider hiring an attorney.

10) **Receiving government files**: The Freedom of Information Act gives every American the right to receive copies of government information about him or her. Write a letter to the appropriate state or federal agency, noting the precise information you want. List each document in a separate paragraph. Mention the Freedom of Information Act, and state that you will pay any expenses. Close with your signature and the address the documents should be sent to. An approved request may take six months to arrive. If it is refused on the grounds that the information is classified or violates another's privacy, send a letter of appeal explaining why the released information would not endanger anyone. Enlist the support of your local state or federal representative, if possible, to smooth the approval process.

11) **Citizenship**: Arriving in the United States to work and become a citizen is a process tangled in bureaucratic red tape, but it requires more perseverance than legal assistance. Immigrants can learn how to obtain a "Green Card," under what circumstances they can work, and what the requirements of citizenship are by contacting the Immigration Services or reading a good self-help book.

Save more; it's E-Z

When it comes to saving attorneys' fees, E-Z Legal Forms is the consumer's best friend. America's largest publisher of self-help legal products offers legally valid forms for virtually every situation. E-Z Legal Kits and E-Z Legal Guides include all necessary forms with a simple-to-follow manual of instructions or a layman's book. E-Z Legal Books are a legal library of forms and documents for everyday business and personal needs. E-Z Legal Software provides those same forms on disk and CD for customized documents at the touch of the keyboard.

You can add to your legal savvy and your ability to protect yourself, your loved ones, your business and your property with a range of self-help legal titles available through E-Z Legal Forms. See the product descriptions and information at the back of this guide.

BE INFORMED —
PROTECTED!

The E-Z Legal
Sexual Harassment Poster

If you do not have a well-communicated sexual harassment policy, you are vulnerable to employee lawsuits for sexual harassment.

Give your employees the information they need and protect your company from needless harassment suits by placing this poster wherever you hang your labor law poster.

BONUS! Receive our helpful manual *How to Avoid Sexual Harassment Lawsuits* with your purchase of the Sexual Harassment Poster.

See the order form in this guide, and order yours today!

FEDERAL & STATE
Labor Law Posters

State	Item#	State	Item#	State	Item#
Alabama	83801	Louisiana	83818	Ohio	83835
Alaska	83802	Maine	83819	Oklahoma	83836
Arizona	83803	Maryland	83820	Oregon	83837
Arkansas	83804	Massachusetts	83821	Pennsylvania	83838
California	83805	Michigan	83822	Rhode Island	83839
Colorado	83806	Minnesota	83823	South Carolina	83840
Connecticut	83807	Mississippi	83824	*South Dakota not available*	
Delaware	83808	Missouri	83825	Tennessee	83842
Florida	83809	Montana	83826	Texas	83843
Georgia	83810	Nebraska	83827	Utah	83844
Hawaii	83811	Nevada	83828	Vermont	83845
Idaho	83812	New Hampshire	83829	Virginia	83846
Illinois	83813	New Jersey	83830	Washington	83847
Indiana	83814	New Mexico	83831	Washington, D.C.	83848
Iowa	83815	New York	83832	West Virginia	83849
Kansas	83816	North Carolina	83833	Wisconsin	83850
Kentucky	83817	North Dakota	83834	Wyoming	83851

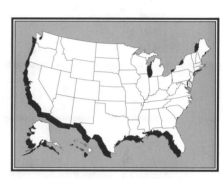

ss1999.r1

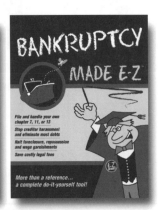

Index

T-W ••••••